Love Through The Eyes
of a Seventeen Year Old

Author

Anonymous

Love Through The Eyes of a Seventeen Year Old

The characters and the story in this book are fiction.

www.chelseasongbird.com

Printed in the United States of America

Library of Congress Control Number: 2011915835

ISBN 978-0-9846217-0-5

Introduction

This book is a continuation of Love Through The Eyes of a Sixteen Year Old. Chelsea has feelings for two different boys. One she has kissed, the other doesn't know who she is in the beginning. As time goes on she realizes she has a crush on two boys. Not a good situation.

Acknowledgments

I would like to dedicate this book to all 17 year old teens, especially Britty Rae.

www.chelseasongbird.com

Table of Contents

Chapter 1
The Headbangers

The Headbangers performance at the Under 17 U.S. Women's National Team is soon to come to an end. We all will soon be joining the Under 20 Women's Championship. We had a great time playing with the Spring Tide at the Under 17 U.S. Women's National Team even though we lost to the Hurricane Force, in the first soccer game we ever played in. As the team learned to play together, we became unbeatable.

Myself, BreAnna, Angela and Sara refer to ourselves as the Headbangers because the first soccer move we mastered was heading the ball. This is where you hit the ball with the flat part of your forehead. You see, unless you are the goaltender, you are not allowed to catch the ball with your hands, so you use your head at that height.

On July 25th I will turn seventeen and that is just a week away. The Headbangers were the oldest teens on the Spring Tide team and that could be why we were a force to be reckoned with. I wonder what it will be like to be on a team where we will be the youngest players.

The Headbangers decided to take this last week off before I turn seventeen, from playing soccer with the Spring Tide, so we can scout out the Under 20 Women's team that would best fit our interest. Some of the teams we observed were not even as good as most of the Under 17 teams. Saturday morning, the day before my birthday we discovered the team that we all wanted to be a part of. Their name is the Elite Kickers. What got our interest was their speed. Soccer is ruled by speed and eye foot coordination and these females are really quick. We want to be noticed and this team is a perfect fit for our agenda.

After the Elite Kickers game was over, all four of us went to the coach and asked if we could join the team. He said for us to come to practice on Monday and he would let us know. We were excited and wanted to show the coach what we had to offer. If he takes us to be part of the team we will have three years to play with the same team members, which will make us a powerful force in the world of soccer.

The Headbangers now have a reason to celebrate the possible chance to be on the team of the Elite Kickers, that is, if we can impress the coach. BreAnna suggested we have seafood and everyone was in complete agreement. We toasted our glasses of tea to our future for the next three years in soccer. We are very optimistic about becoming part of the team.

Suddenly the waiters were all around our table and began singing, "Happy Birthday Chelsea," this must be BreAnna's idea. A cake was placed in the middle of the table with 17 burning candles. BreAnna said, "Make a wish and blow them out before they burn up the cake." I took a deep breath and under that breath I said to myself, "Please let the coach take all four of us for the soccer team." With that I blew out all 17 candles. When I looked up, there was Zack, Kyle, Jake and Brad clapping their hands. I said, "This is great, you guys surprised me, I had no idea this was going to happen. You're the best!" The guys were in the restaurant the whole time and I didn't even notice them. They were pretty slick. We all had some cake and Zack offered to take me home. Zack and myself had a long conversation about the past year and how Jeff's accident on the football field with that faulty helmet changed my life. I told Zack about how Jeff's mother told me that Jeff felt uncomfortable talking to me because he did not remember whom I was.

Zack is fully aware that Jeff only recently learned to tie his shoestring. It's a bad situation that has only got worse with time as far as our relationship. Jeff is cutting me out of his life and I am slowly turning lose of him as well. Zack walked me to my door and gave me a big hug and a kiss on the forehead and said happy birthday once again.

I met Jeff last year while on vacation in Florida. We had a strong connection instantly and to this day I visit those feelings in my mind. It was a new feeling for me at the time and sometimes I wonder if that will ever happen to me again. I always refer to it as my first crush but I wonder if it was love. I refer to this in the past tense because it is now just a one way, feeling. Before Jeff's accident he also felt the electric feelings, but has lost memory of them.

The morning light came rushing through my window and there was a nock on my bedroom door. I said, "Come in," and in through the door came my mom and dad with a stack of banana pancakes and seventeen candles of fire. They sang happy birthday and I blew out the candles.

Breakfast in bed is one of my favorite things in life. These pancakes had bananas cooked inside of the pancake and warm honey in a separate container that I poured around the side of the pancakes so I could dip each bite in for just the right amount of honey. Every bite is truly delicious to my taste and smell. My mom is a great cook. Dad handed me an envelope and as I opened it they began to sing happy birthday. Inside the card was a one hundred dollar bill. This is perfect because gas for my Mustang is getting higher all the time. I gave mom and dad a hug and dad took my breakfast tray and out the door they went.

I got dressed and checked my E-Mail to see if my sister Cloie sent me any mail. Sure enough she did. What she said was, "Russia sure is cold but thinking of you having a birthday warms my soul. Wish I could be there. Matt also says have a great day." My sister is great, and Jeff's brother, Matt is perfect for her. They make a beautiful married couple.

Jeff's mother and his brother Ed also wished me a happy birthday in E-Mail form. It's nice to know they remembered. I spent the day with my parent's and it was wonderful. They always spoil me on my birthday. We went for a drive in the country and out to eat. It's so neat to spend the day with them and hear the story about how I came into existence. Mom swears she knows the exact moment that I was conceived. That is when her egg and dad's sperm were united, and I first existed. Mom says it was a cold November Sunday when she and dad decided to get some R&R. They always refer to their R&R as Religion, which is going to church in the morning, and romance, which is making love in the evening. Mom circled the day on the calendar that I was conceived, and nine months later I was born. Mom put the page out of the calendar in my baby book, which she started that very day. It's hard to deny the facts when they are in your face. Hopefully when I start my family, I also will know when the very moment my child is conceived.

I love the drives in the country where I get a chance to see areas of land for the first time. It has such a sense of new to me. We passed by a horse ranch where people were training their horses for racing with a track and a release gate facility. Dad pulled the car over and we got out and watched. These were thoroughbreds, a cross of Arabian stallions with English mares. They were released from the gate just as we got to the fence. The track looked to be a mile long and these horses were very competitive. They looked each other in the eye, as if to say, 'I'm going to beat you.' I could see that they love racing and it is bringing joy into what would be a boring day of just eating grass for the horses. I could see the competitive nature in their eye. I recognize it because I have a very competitive nature myself. It makes life exciting.

These well bread horses are truly beautiful to watch. Both think they won the race because they were strutting around like, 'I'm the one.' It was a very close race, but I'm sure one won by a nose length. Seldom is there a tie in horse racing. The jock's waved at us and we waved back. Everyone was having a great time. It's sad to think that anyone would want to take this great sport away from the horses or the owners. It would be cruel not let these competitive horses compete for which one is the best. Life is full of chances and accidents. A horse could be in a pasture alone, and step in a gopher hole and break it's leg. Anything can happen, lets just hope if it does they are doing what brings them joy when and if it does happen. I would hate to think people weren't allowed to drive cars because some people die in car accident. Horses should be able to enjoy a good race, it's in their blood, and nature.

The second group of horses entered the gate and I told my dad that I liked the big brown horse with a black main and tail. Dad said, "He's a beauty." The gate opened and as they raced past us some of the dirt flew in my face. These horses were really moving. On the second trip around the track the horse I liked was a whole body length ahead. He won the race and my dad gave me a thumb's up.

Monday morning BreAnna called and said she would be by to pick me up in an hour. We were meeting the coach of the Elite Kickers to see if he would let us join the team. When BreAnna pulled up in front of my house she had Sara and Angela already in the car. I got in and said, "Well Headbangers are you ready to show off your stuff?" Each went in a detailed description of the moves they plan to use to impress the coach. I must say, if excitement is part of what the coach is looking for, than we are a shoe in.

As we were walking towards the field the coach recognized us and waved us towards him. This is a good sign, a warm reception, he remembers us. BreAnna put her hand out for the coach to get introduced and said, "My name is BreAnna, and this is Chelsea, Angela, and Sara." The coach shook each of our hands and welcomed us to the field. He introduced his self as coach Ross, threw us a ball and said, "Show me what you have to offer." Immediately we started heading the ball to each other. That put a smile on coach Ross's face. Next each of us bounced the ball on our knee and onto our foot. What we were trying to display was our ability to control the ball. The coach started clapping his hands and said, "Very impressive. Let's see what you got on the field. One of you girls take the position of goalkeeper and the others try to score on her." BreAnna immediately took her position as goalkeeper and we began kicking the ball towards the net. BreAnna was doing a great job of keeping the ball out of the net when I did a header that she tipped with her finger but it went in anyway. After all I have to show off my skills as well. This went on for ten minutes. Normally the other team would be keeping the ball from going anywhere near the goalkeeper, but coach Ross wanted to see what BreAnna had to offer. He blew his whistle and told us to go get a bottle of water out of the ice chest and take a break. He called over his assisting coach and they went over his notes. We watched the team practice while the coaches continued to talk about us. Finally coach Ross motioned for us to come over, anyway we though he wanted all of us but he said, "Only BreAnna." BreAnna turned to us and said, "I'll be right back."

My heart fell to my feet at the thought that BreAnna may be the only one the coach wanted for his team. We all know what an important position goalkeeping is and BreAnna is very good at keeping the ball out of the net. I will be happy for her even if I'm not chosen to be on the team. It never crossed my mind that the coach only wants one of us for his team until now. The coach was sharing his notes with BreAnna and she was pointing at his clipboard and telling him what she thought. I thought they would never stop talking, when suddenly coach Ross turned and pointed at me. BreAnna started walking towards us and said, "Coach Ross wants to see you Chelsea." My heart started beating out of my chest. I don't know why I have so much trouble controlling my emotions.

When I finally made it to where the coaches were, they were talking and I began to regain my composure. A big smile came across my face and I said, "You wanted to talk to me." Coach Ross said, "Indeed I do young lady. Your friend BreAnna is one of the most talented goalkeepers I've ever seen in my life. She is what we call a natural. I see a lot of potential in you as well. You seem to have the ability to read a players next move. In the game of soccer that is very important. You were the only one to score on BreAnna. Soccer is a very low scoring game, as you know, so making a goal is what it's all about. You are on the team."

I'm so excited, as I walked back towards the Headbangers, the coach motioned for Angela and Sara. I nodded to BreAnna and it was understood that I also was on the team. We both crossed our fingers as Angela and Sara walked the long walk towards the coaches. Both spent way longer talking to coach Ross than me, or BreAnna did. This is not a good sign. If they don't make the team it just won't be the same.

Coach Ross made a sign with his hand for BreAnna and myself to join in the conversation. We put our water bottles down and joined the group. Coach Ross asked us to play against each other. He called out to his goalkeeper to practice with us. He had Sara and Angela play the position of guarding the ball from going into the net and BreAnna and myself would be trying to make a goal. Angela was doing some fancy footwork with the ball and Sara was shining with her ability to knee the ball. Neither of us could make a goal, but it is three against two. After 10 minutes the coach said to take a break and drink some water. It's turning into a very hot day and the water is so refreshing. This time he took 30 minutes to call us back to talk. He motioned for all of us to join him and his assistant coach. He started off like this, "I see potential in all of you to become great soccer players, however only one is a natural, and that is BreAnna. The rest of you can develop into a force to be reckoned with as BreAnna so elegantly told me, so be here at 9:00am tomorrow to start practicing with the Elite Kickers."

BreAnna talked us up good to coach Ross and she could tell we knew it. We all gave her a pat on the back as we squealed with joy. We have a chance to prove ourselves to be Headbangers of the future. We know what our talents are, so now we have the opportunity to show others what we are made of.

The first thing I did when I got home was to call Zack and tell him the good news. He knew how important it was to the Headbangers to be able to all play on the same team, and he was excited for us. Zack said he would be right over and that we could celebrate my making the team. When he arrived, he had a sack with two gyro wraps and two, ice tea's. The gyros were made of lamb with a cucumber sauce, tomato's, onion and lettuce all wrapped in flat bread. This is one of my favorite sandwiches.

Zack gave me a hug and suggested we go out on the backyard patio to eat our lunch. It is a beautiful summer day and I always prefer eating outside when the weather is permitting. We talked about how fast time was moving. Part of the reason was because we haven't spent as much time together as in the past. Zack is playing baseball this summer and with my job at the mall, and playing soccer, both are taking up a lot of my time. We just miss spending time together.

Zack grabbed a couple of float's and then my hand and we headed for the pond. He said, "We need to soak up some sun." As we were walking to the pond, Bam suddenly was walking right behind us. She came out of nowhere. When Zack seen Bam he said, "That deer is getting fat, or she is carrying a doe." I said, "Something is going on with her, that's for sure." Zack gave Bam a scratch behind her ear and said, "Way to go Bam."

The water felt great. Because we had just eaten lunch, we just floated on the water and had some heart to heart talks. It feels great to be able to share my inter most feelings with Zack, he is such a good listener.

I started off talking about how soccer brought back joy in my life. The year has basically been a haze since Jeff's accident. At first I thought he would never wake up. When he did wake up, he had no idea who I was and just wanted me to go away. I think being young made all of this more difficult to deal with. However, soccer gave me back my ability to get past all the sorrow my heart was felling. It gave me a reason to be excited about life once again.

Zack is a great listener and I adore that quality in him. Sometimes I have crazy insecurities and Zack helps me get control of them. I did not know how to chase away the pain associated with Jeff's accident until Zack kissed me and soccer became a part of my life. Actually, I kissed Zack, he came near my lips, but my head moved to make contact, and that means I kissed him. The combination of Zack's kiss and soccer brought me out of a year long, sadness. It's strange how an event can control our minds for such a long time.

While floating on the pond I reached deep down into my soul and laid it out for Zack to see. I told him, "Jeff is finally a part of my past. The memory of what we had will always be part of me, but Jeff is no longer that person. He has morphed into a stranger who I no longer recognize. Jeff's mother told me that he doesn't want to hear my name ever again. My name strikes fear in him and he is unable to deal with the feelings. Jeff thinks that God is leading him. He told his mom, "I'm either letting God led me, or I'm being led by the flesh." Right now Jeff claims that God's love elevates him to a state of comfort in which he wishes to remain. He told his mother that to go down the path of evil is not fulfilling, you must ask God to transform you to walk in his light with all that is good. Jeff has given his whole life to God and wants no distractions.

Jeff will never regain his motor skills 100% but he can manage with what he has. His brother Ed has devoted his life to take Jeff to church and to social functions where Jeff feels comfortable. They feed off of each others energy."

After unloading all these emotions suddenly everything seemed brighter, the grass was greener the water blue as a morning glory flower, and the yellow daises were as bright as the sun. Zack could see the transformation in me and gave me a wink. He grabbed my hand and gave it a gentle squeeze. Not another word was said as we floated on the pond in total bliss. There was a sense of closure in the air that did not require words.

Zack stayed for a while longer and left only because he had baseball practice. Then BreAnna called and invited me to stay overnight, which shortly after our conversation I was on my way to her house.

When I pulled up, BreAnna was bouncing a soccer ball on her knee. I got out of the car and BreAnna bounced the ball off her knee and jumped up with her other foot to strike the ball in my direction with the side of her foot. I caught it with my forehead and with that header hit the ball breezed right past BreAnna's hands. BreAnna said, "We can use that move to make some scores, it's perfect. I had to show it to you, and you knew exactly what to do with the ball without me having to explain it to you."

We continued to practice this move for 30 minutes and then it was time for a drink of water. The heat demanded that we take a break.

BreAnna said, "I've been working on that move for a

week. It's so quick the other team won't even see it coming. This move could make us famous, I'm so excited."

BreAnna could have something, the move she has come up with is very tricky, the goalkeeper will think it's going to be a kick at one end of the net but the forward hits it with their forehead and it goes in the opposite side of the net. It's a perfect strategy.

BreAnna's mother called for us to come to supper. Fried chicken, mashed potato's, gravy, and green bean's were on the table. I cleaned the wishbone from the chicken and put it in BreAnna's face. She grabbed the other end, we waited for a moment so each could make a wish in their head, and began to pull it apart. BreAnna just smiled as she came up with the winning end of the bone. She is smiling with satisfaction at her ability to win once again. There's no way she will tell me what she wished, for that would jeopardize the wish coming true. For desert we had peach cobbler. BreAnna let me know she picked the peaches off their tree this morning and her mother cooked the cobbler this morning. The peach cobbler was still warm, and delicious is the word to describe this cobbler.

After dinner we went upstairs, to BreAnna's room, to listen to some music. She asked me what was going on with Jeff. I began with, "Strange you should ask, Zack came by to visit earlier today and we talked about Jeff, it's more like I talked about Jeff. I received an E-Mail from Jeff's mother the other day and she shared some of Jeff's concerns with me. Jeff said, with a tear in his voice, "God gave me the will to live, and I've seen the purpose of my life because I've seen death, but I survived. I want to dedicate my life to sharing what I know about God with those who doubt His existence. The preciousness of life has opened my eyes and I want to share that. Because of my accident, my brother Ed has his life back. That is a gift that came out of a tragedy. I have a love for God that gives me energy, a very powerful energy. Everybody needs a fresh start and because of me, Ed is dedicating his life to me so I may serve God. Together we will reach drug addicts and pull them from the hell they are in and show them they to can get a fresh start in life." When it was put to me like that, I was able to share Jeff's thoughts and be happy for him. He will make an impact on this world and drive away the evils of addiction that plague our country. Addiction has become a fatal epidemic disease that will be the ruination of our country.

The road that Jeff has chosen is so like him only in high gear. Ed has joined Jeff's crusade and together they will make a difference. Ed had his demon in the world of drugs and he knows it is possible to stop. He will be able to reach these people because at one time he was one of them. Ed knows that if a drug addict can find a reason to quit, it is possible to quit and get a fresh start, but they must have a reason to want to quit.

I feel privileged to know Jeff, for he showed me a side of life that can bring great pleasure to the heart and soul. He is a good person, the kind I hope to find again in life and make a family with. After all, family is what makes life good.

Ed has woken up from his drug-induced life and his eyes are now open to the importance of finding a soul mate. He is aware that the person you share your life with will provide heaven or hell on earth. Ed believes your mind is your world or your world is your mind. However you choose to look at it. He will start his family with this belief and is in search for his happiness. He sent me E-Mail just the other day, to tell me that this beautiful woman continually makes small talk with him. This woman touches Ed's arm and tries to get him off to herself, but Ed knows she would be trouble for him. She is so beautiful he would want to lock her in a room where he would not have to share her with anyone. Beautiful women have this effect on Ed and he knows it. Being with a beautiful woman would be self-destructive for

Ed just like the drugs were. He knows this and refuses to put himself in harms way. His marriage to an ugly woman with a good heart and personality is his ultimate goal in life." With all that conversation, I went to sleep.

The next morning BreAnna called Angela and Sara to ask them to come to her house for some Headbanging practice. She wants to share the new move with the knee, foot and head. When they arrived, BreAnna is cooking some oatmeal with honey and cinnamon. She added just a touch of milk. On the side we had a piece of toast with black currant jelly. With BreAnna it's all about energy food that gives you quickness. She claims it is the secret to winning, that and talent.

While we were eating breakfast Sara started talking about a guy who has a cup of coffee and a muffin every day for breakfast at the restaurant where she works. Sara talked about how handsome he is and how he always leaves a tip. This kind of talk has all of us sitting up taller and hanging on every word Sara is saying.

BreAnna couldn't help herself, she blurted out, "What about Kyle, aren't you two an item." Sara said, "We are great friends, and yes we do care about each other, but BreAnna, we are nothing like you and Jake. We are not, in love, we are in a great friendship. It's okay if we decide to date someone else. As a matter of fact the guy at the restaurant, Nick, has asked me to meet him at the theater so we can go to a movie together." I suddenly said, "Why does he want to meet you there, why doesn't he pick you up?" Sara said, "He wants to start out slow and get to know each other before we start dating. He wants to start out just sharing experiences. He drives a red Corvette and looks so hot driving up to the restaurant with his sunglasses on." Angela said, "Yea, he's to cool for us, Sara has asked him if he would like to go to one of our gatherings and he said, 'I don't need to make any more friends, I just want to get to know you', yea right."

BreAnna said, "Enough already, let's go practice our new moves for soccer. We have a game next week and this move is sure to put points on the board."

Sara has been acting different lately, now I know what the cause is. This guy Nick is distracting Sara. I've never seen her in this kind of a haze before. I thought she just wasn't feeling well. She certainly hasn't been her socialite self lately. This person named Nick has changed Sara's personality. Deep inside of my gut, something tells me this guy is not good for Sara.

In two hours time we all got the new move down to a science. Each vowed to practice the new move until it was second nature. My dad made me a make shift net that was the size of the official net used in games. It was made from plastic plumbing, and netting he used for catching fish. I must have put the ball into my make shift goal at least 100 times in the past week. I'm ready for whatever the next team we play has to offer.

Zack invited me, and our friends to his first baseball game. It's still daylight but this game will go on into the night. The ball field already has the lights on so the darkness that is nearing won't be a problem. It's time for a hotdog and a bottle of water. We want to be in our seats before the game begins. These hotdogs are 100% beef and I top mine with mustard and sweet relish. Each of my friends said, 'The same,' as they came to the counter to order.

Just as we all finished our hotdogs it was time for the National Anthem, to sound out our allegiance to our great nation. I love this part of sports. There is just something about everyone saying the same thing at one time. We have the greatest nation on earth and this reminds all of us, of the greatness we share. It just fills my heart with joy.

The game is beginning and a retired Baseball professional player is on the pitchers mound to throw the ceremonial first pitch. Everyone is on there feet clapping in honor of his presence. He has provided many years of entertainment for millions of baseball fans. The continuous clapping is this town's way of saying thank you for all the years of joy he has brought to us.

As the professional Baseball player leaves the pitching mound, Zack shakes his hand and takes his place on the pitchers mound and the game begins. Zack's first pitch to the Python's is a low ball and it is strike one. Zack's second pitch is a high ball and it is strike two. Next Zack throws a curve ball and the Python player is out with strike three. Zack continued to throw balls that the Python's bat just could not connect on. Now it's time for the Falcon's to try to hit the ball. It's Zack's turn and there is a Falcon on second and third base. The Python pitcher is very impressed with Zack's ability to pitch and he is not wanting Zack to be able to hit any of his pitches so he would through to the outside to just walk Zack. Now the bases are loaded. The pressure is on for the next Falcon batter. He is holding the bat up high, this way he can swing with great momentum and the velocity of the ball when hit, will fly out of the ballpark. The Python pitcher threw the first ball and it was ball one; that went behind the batter. The next pitch was a ball two, just left of the plate. The Falcon batter is rocking back and forth from one foot, than to the other. The pitcher than throws a ball high and it is called, ball three. Next the pitcher throws a low ball and the Falcon batter swings with everything he has and catches it on the tip of his bat and it flies plum out of the ballpark. It's a home run and all three basses are running in. What a jaw dropping hit it was. Everybody in the ballpark is on there feet. The roar of the crowd is deafening. The Falcons have made the kind of play that will be talked about for years in this little town.

As Zack ran across the home plate, I hollered, 'You go Zack,' even though I knew he couldn't hear me. The crowd is so loud I can't even hear my own voice. The four runs on this play is what made the Falcon's win the game. Zack threw another no hitter inning and is now the town hero. The Pythons never even put a single point on the board. That's how good a pitcher Zack is this particular night. He may never do this again, but he did do it tonight.

The game is over and the fans are descending on the field. Zack sees me and he grabs me around my waist and swings me in a circle. The rest of our friends surround Zack and me and are jumping up and down with excitement and joy of the Falcons win. Our friends are saying, "This calls for a celebration." Zack's mom and dad are patting all of us on the back and hollering louder than anyone else in the crowd. After all Zack is their son and they are very proud of what he has done tonight.

Zack is way to tired to celebrate tonight and suggested we go to a drive in movie tomorrow night. Zack is wanting to see a new western movie that has a four star ratting. We all agreed. Zack asked if I would come by his house in an hour and just hang out. He needed time to take a shower and talk to his family about the awesome win the Falcons had tonight. As Zack walked me to my car, the aromatic fragrant of his leather glove and baseball filed my senses. All the oils are releasing the sweet-smelling aroma that leather gets when it is used. Zack is very excited about the win and it shows in his voice. It's like he is super charged.

Zack doesn't live far from me so I decided to take a quick shower. Before the sun went down it was very hot and my skin is very sticky. When I walked in the front door dad said, "I heard on the news that the Falcon's won their game tonight. Zack's arm must have been strong tonight to shut out the Python's. They are a good team you know. Next time you see Zack, tell him I'm proud of him. Will ya?" "I'll tell him tonight, I'm going to take a quick shower and go by his house for a little while. He asked me over to just hang out," I said.

When I pulled up to Zack's house he was sitting on the front porch swing and immediately got up to open my car door. He grabbed my hand and we walked side by side up the steps to the swing. Before we sat down Zack gave me a hug that lasted at least a full minute. He rocked side to side and talked about what a blast he had playing baseball tonight. He told me he was glad I came to watch him play. As I sat down on the swing Zack handed me a tall glass of lemonade. It really hit the spot. Zack said, "You know Chelsea, baseball is such a cool game. You don't have to be tall, super strong, or even very fast. There is a position for most anyone to play. I'm just lucky I have an arm for throwing the ball. I like playing all positions, but the coach thinks that pitcher is my strongest position in the game. I may never shut out another team in my life, but I did shut out the Python's tonight. It's so exciting." I said, "Yes it's very exciting and I can feel your joy right now. You were awesome tonight, and in my books you made history tonight. I will always remember this game."

Zack looked up at the sky and said, "You know Chelsea, people who live in the city don't get to see the stars the way country people do. They are so bright tonight that they look like jewels. They are all sparkly, and full with excitement, just like me. You know the stars, moons, and plants must have lined up just right for me to have thrown the ball so perfect that I shut out the Python's." I said, "Let me feel that arm that brought stardom to the Falcon's tonight. Yes if I must say so myself, that is a very strong arm. Make a muscle for me, yes indeed that is some arm you have Zack." We laughed and both looked up at the stars for a good long while before we spoke again. I love these silent moments when our minds just enjoy being together without any sound. We are so in tune with each other that silence feels good instead of awkward. Zack grabbed my hand and I felt his energy. I'm happy for his excitement.

It is getting late and Zack began to doze off, so I broke the silence and said that it is time for me to go home. Zack walked me to my car, kissed my forehead, and thanked me for being with him tonight. I told him that I would be seeing him tomorrow.

I'm glad Zack lives close because I'm very sleepy. All the excitement has drained my energy. I fell on the bed and went out like a light. Next thing I knew, my mom was knocking on my door and asking me to join her and dad for breakfast. Orange juice and an omelet were on the table for me. I wolfed them down like I hadn't eaten in days. Mom said, "Slow down no one's going to take that from you." I said, "It's just so good I couldn't help myself. The onions and bell peppers have just the right crunch to them. Delicious and delightful describes this breakfast. Thanks mom for getting me up, soccer practice starts in an hour and I need to swing by and pick up BreAnna, her car needs a new battery. She doesn't get paid until next week so I'm giving her a ride."

BreAnna was ready and waiting in the driveway for me. She was bouncing her soccer ball on her knee, than her head, then back on her knee. It's like she can't stand still. The mornings are cool but by 1:00 o'clock the sun starts taking it's toll. Our coach stops practice at 12:00 noon to be sure we don't get in trouble with the heat. Today we practiced putting the ball behind our left foot and bringing it back to the front with our right foot. It is a tedious move that is tiresome due to the slowness. It's very awkward but necessary to perfect. It can keep you from getting the ball stolen from under your foot. By the time practice was over we all had it down to a fine art.

On the way home from soccer practice, BreAnna suggested that we double date tonight at the outdoor movie. Angela and Sara are taking Sara's car so they can double date and park next to us. Sounds like a lot of fun so I told BreAnna to be ready by 8 o'clock and have Jake at her house. We can get there a little early to be sure we can park next to each other.

I took my car because we couldn't all fit in Zack's truck. He was okay with me driving and I thought that was so cool. Zack doesn't have to be in control all the time. I like that. Our cars are positioned in the center of the outdoor Drive-Inn movie picture. We all get out of our cars and talk for a while before the movie starts. Brad held up a tee shirt that had little sayings from each of us about Zack's pitching ability with our names signed under each comment. The writing that I signed my name to read, 'staying power,' this is because Zack pitched the entire game without getting a replacement pitcher. This is unheard of. BreAnna and Jake had a pitcher of a muscle arm with their names under the arm and 'Zack,' printed on the muscle of the arm. Angela and Brad had 'shut them out,' printed on the tee shirt with Angela's name on top and Brad's name underneath. Zack was so excited. He gave each of us a hug. We talked about the game for another 30 minutes, and then it was time for the movie to begin.

The name of the movie is 'Wanted Poster.' The movie started with a gunfight in a saloon. Six cowboys were sitting at the round table playing cards when two of them jumped up and accused one of the players of cheating. The accused cheater bit down on his cigar and claimed he did not need to cheat, and that he never played such dumb cow-pokers in his life. He had a gun under the table and shot one in the kneecap and the other in the leg before they even knew what happened. As they were falling to the ground they fired their guns hitting innocent bystanders. The man playing the piano was shot in the back and died instantly. The other was a saloon girl who was hit in the shoulder. A third man that was playing cards jumped up and kicked the guns out of the hands of the two men on the floor who had been shot before they could shot anyone else. The forth man who had been chewing on a cigar and had been accused of cheating jumped up and told one of the injured men that he was going to kill him. He cocked his gun and than the man, who had kicked the guns out of the injured men's hands, shot the cigar chewing man right between the eyes. It all happened so fast that the third gunman walked out of the saloon backwards with his gun still drawn. This made him look guilty even though he was protecting an unarmed man. In his mind a judge should decide if this man should be found guilty, not a cigar chewing card player. After he shot the man with the cigar everyone was looking at him like he was a cold-blooded killer, he could see this in his or her eyes. He panicked and fled the scene.

When the sheriff arrived there were five different stories about the way things came down. The sheriff decided that the only way to sort this out is for a judge to decide, guilty or not guilty. The sheriff gathered a description of the gunman and had an artist put together a Wanted Poster.

The man, who shot the cigar chewing card player between the eyes, name is Bart, but no one in the town knew his name. The Wanted Poster just has a sketch of his face. Bart acted on his instincts to protect; a strong impulse made him act before thoughts of the outcome could be analyzed.

Bart is a drifter who works for different cattle drivers. He likes seeing the country and getting paid for it at the same time. Bart was in this New Mexico town looking for work. He's not a bad man, things just got out of hand. Bart panicked when he shot the man and his fight and flight adrenaline kicked in, you see he never shot a person before. Bart is only nineteen years old and lost his parents when he was fourteen to a wild bear attract. Bart climbed a tree or he would have died that day with his parents. He basically raised himself by doing odd jobs for people to earn enough money to buy a horse. By the time he was fifteen he was herding cattle to wherever the market was for them. It was a life he loved. Now he is running scared, not sure if a posse, a group of persons deputized by a sheriff to aid in law enforcement, is looking for him. You see, the man he shot lived in the town and was some kind of a big shot cattle rancher. Bart was planning on asking for a job before he killed the man.

Bart rode his horse until both were so tired they had to stop. A tree on top of a hill looks like a good stopping place. This way, Bart can see if anyone is chasing after him. When Bart dismounts from his horse, he takes off his hat and drops to his knees and begins to cry. He puts his hand over his face and says out loud, "What have I done, what have I done." He is so upset that he begins to throw up, three times before he can stop. He can't seem to get control of himself. His horse nudges him as if to comfort his sorrow. He falls to the ground covering his face and begins screaming into his hands. He is totally out of control.

The horse begins to look uneasy and Bart gathers himself up to look around and see why his horse is backing up. Below is a posse of around twenty people heading in Bart's direction. They look to be an hour away and soon it will be nightfall. Bart and his horse will rest for a while longer before they start their journey to Colorado. Bart knows this country well and has a friend who lives in the mountains. He met her after a long cattle drive on a winter day. She told him he is welcome anytime. Her name is Lucy and she lives alone. She pans for gold and finds enough to make a living. It is a good two-day ride to her place and Bart will sleep in a cave tonight and get a good start in the early morning. His emotions are running from remorse for what he did, to fear that the posse is going to catch up to him. Being hunted is the ultimate fear that a man can experience. Especially when it is twenty men on horseback. Sleep is not sound for Bart tonight. He has blankets and water so comfort is not the problem, it's the fear that fills his mind and has him waking up all through the night. At daybreak he mounts his horse and begins his journey slowly so his horse does not get tired. His plan is to keep moving in a northerly direction, until night falls once again.

Bart finds a heavy patch of cactus and starts to cut them open for their moisture. It is a tedious task because of all the stickers on the cactus. He has a cup for himself and a pan for his horse. Bart scrapes all the insides out of the cactus and puts them in a handkerchief and squeezes to extract the liquid. He continues to do this until he has two full cups for the horse, and a half-cup for himself. The water in his canteen needs to be saved for the hottest part of the day.

Hungry for food Bart's stomach is growling loud enough for the posse to hear. Bart sees a lizard and the race is on. The lizard is darting left than right, like a zigzag pattern. Suddenly it disappears down a hole. Bart begins digging with his hands, than his knife as the lizards tail appears and disappears in the hole. Bart is gaining on the lizard and grabs a foot. He holds him in the air and says, "Your going to be my lunch." Bart cleans the intestines out of the lizard and eats it raw. Everyone began to squirm and wiggled in a snakelike motion as Bart crunched on the bones of the lizard. We could hear Angela say, "That is just nasty." BreAnna said, "He could have at least cooked it."

Bart leads his horse Daisy to a patch of dry grass. Daisy didn't care that it was dry; she just wanted something to eat. A grasshopper jumps and Bart grabs it and pop's it in his mouth. He mumbles, "Taste like a chew of tobacco." Jake said, "This guy will eat anything." Brad said, "Keep it down over there, we are trying to watch the movie." We could all tell by the chuckle in his voice, he was just messing with us. Zack grabbed my hand and said, "Does that make you hungry." I elbowed him in the side and said, "Gross."

Bart talks to his horse Daisy all the time. He mumbles things like, "I wish we had some supplies, like food and more water, you know, like when we go on a cattle drive, we always have what we need. I didn't plan on killing a man and running for my life from a twenty-man posse. Old girl if it looks like they are going to get me, I'll set you loses and you run like the wind. You go find yourself a nice family to live with. Your pretty enough that anyone will take you in to be part of their family."

I guess if you're a loaner like Bart, you need to just talk sometimes. When you drift from one job to another, your best friend would be your horse. You have only temporary friends. Most of this movie has Bart talking to his horse. The best part is when he begins to reminisce about how he met Lucy.

"Daisy you know if it weren't for you I never would have met Lucy. That snowy morning when I came out of that saloon and seen Lucy petting you, with the ugly old Mule of hers tied up next to you, I thought Lucy was the prettiest thing I had ever seen. It was like I should be ridding that old Mule and she should be ridding you. I imaged Lucy being like Lady Gadiver, ridding on you with all that beautiful blonde hair covering her nude body. Here I'm looking as ugly as that old Mule she rides, didn't think I had a chance of even talking to her. I just watched Lucy as she brushed the snow off your back and told you how beautiful you are. You sure took her. When I walked up to the both of you and she smiled and asked, "Is she your horse?" I got the chills. That smile was like a ray of sunshine, brightening up a gloomy day. When she offered me that gold nugget to buy you from me, I hated to break her heart by saying no, but I just couldn't part with you. You know Daisy, money is not that big of a thing to me. I like working and I make enough to take care of us, but Lucy thinks different. She wants lots of money and she thinks money will buy her whatever she wants. She is wrong about that. I wouldn't have sold you for a duffle bag of gold. I don't think I could even find another horse that enjoyed me talking to them like you do."

Daisy's ears perked up and she began wenning and nickering and backing up. Bart knew something was wrong and suddenly out of the corner of his eye he seen a snake. It's forked tongue wiggling as it goes in and out of its mouth. It's curling up like it's getting into position to strike. The rattler on its tail begins to shake. If Bart draws his gun to shoot this snake the posse will know his location. Bart just freezes, with sweat dripping off his face. He is frozen, not even blinking an eye when Daisy rares up and smashes the snake with her hoof. Bart looks at her and said, "That's part of why all the gold in Lucy's mountain wouldn't buy you Daisy."

Bart just had a near death situation, whether it would be the posse finding him when they heard the gun shot, or the snake bit, he knew it would be the end of him if it weren't for Daisy. He gave her a hug around the neck and said, "We better get going. Thanks girl."

Bart mounted Daisy and they were off in a slow gallop. Bart wipes the sweat from his forehead, and it was as if the jester was saying 'That was a close one.' They stayed on the move and covered a lot of ground before stopping. A stream of cold mountain water stopped Daisy as she buried her mouth in the stream. Bart lay on the ground and began splashing the water all over his face and neck. He cupped his hands and drank of the cold mountain water until he had his fill. Bart then filled everything that would hold water. The heat was bearing down hard today without clouds in the sky to provide any relief form the sun's rays. Bart glances at the sky as a red tail hawk circles looking for a bite to eat. A crawdad begins to crawl along the bank of the stream and Bart grabs him and pop's his tail off. With his thumbnail he scoops the bite of meat out, and pops it in his mouth. He needs the food for energy. When he left the saloon his stomach was empty except for a couple of beers. They don't sit well with the hot sun. He lost most of it when he threw up at the thought of shooting a man.

Bart and Daisy set off once again heading North to Pagosa, Colorado. The mountain stream is a sure sign they are getting closer to Lucy's cabin. Bart begins to talk about Lucy again. It helps keep his mind off what is really happening and takes him to a much simpler time in his life.

"Lucy sure was taken by you Daisy. When she asked if we had a place to stay for the night, I think she was more concerned about you than she was about me. Lucy knew everyone in town and when I told her we were fixing to ride to the next town because there was no place for us to stay the night, Lucy offered us her barn. First she made us go to the sheriff's office so he could get a look at us in case I was a bad guy and she was found dead the next day. She wanted someone to know who to look for. Lucy is a very wise woman. If I were a bad guy, I would have thought twice before ever harming a hair on her pretty blonde head, with the sheriff knowing what I look like and all.

The barn she put us in was very comfortable with my bed made from hay, and you had all the oats your belly could hold. I think Lucy wanted to take care of you and I just happened to be along for the ride. It would have been a perfect night if it weren't for that mule passing that awful gas all night. He smelled as bad as he looked. What do you think a pretty girl like Lucy is doing with such a despicable creature as that mule? Anyway, the next morning she made the most satisfying meal I've had since mom passed. Every kind of berry you could think of. She had raspberry, blueberry, blackberry, and apricots. She had three pancakes in the middle of the plate stacked on top of each other with honey on each layer, and the berries circled the pancakes. It was so pretty I just looked at it for the longest time. Lucy had to tell me to dig in before the pancakes got cold.

Lucy talked a blue streak before I could get a word in.

She told me all the dreams she had for the future. Lucy is very industrious and for all I know she has already moved on from that little cabin at the foot of the mountain. Whether she is still there or not, we are heading there. I don't know what else to do. I have nowhere to go but there. We just have to hope for the best."

Bart rode for what looked like a long distance and it was time for Daisy to rest. It looks like Bart is very good to his horse by taking it slow and letting her rest as often as possible, or he knows she will last a lot longer and have more endurance in case the posse catches up and they have to bolt. If it comes down to running for your life, I would want my horse to be as fresh as possible.

Bart picked back up on the story about Lucy. Bart began with, "Lucy washed my clothes for me in the stream. She said that the washing was going to have to be done anyway because hers was piling up, but if I wanted to help, I could split some wood for her to cook super with. It seemed like the thing to do. Lucy never said how long we could stay; she just kept cooking and washing my clothes. One evening when we went to town to a barn dance there was a cattle rancher recruiting men for a cattle drive to Ohio. I had never seen Ohio and the itch to go was just overwhelming. The drive was starting in just two days and the excitement filled the town. In just a couple of months you can earn enough money on a cattle drive to last you the rest of the year. Many of the men had families and this would really help them get ahead. Daisy we could use the money ourselves. We could play for the rest of the year."

Bart just had a couple of days to get hired and applied for the job immediately. The rancher told Bart he would be an asset to the drive and made him the boss. All of the experience Bart accumulated on the drives in the past has paid off. Bart was on a high just thinking about the excitement of getting ready for the drive.

Bart said, "You know Daisy, Lucy never made me feel bad about leaving for the cattle drive, but now that I look back, I was so excited about going, that I didn't even think about how Lucy got use to having us around, and maybe her heart was hurting that we were leaving. On the other hand she could be thinking, 'I'm so glad they finally are getting out of here.' Whatever the case, she gave us a hug goodbye, so we are in good standing with her still. Lucy may ask us to leave when I tell her I killed a man, but she will be glad to see us at first.

You know Daisy, Lucy has a good heart and a great personality. Let's don't forget that she is beautiful with long blonde hair and eyes of blue. If she would have just showed some romantic interest we would still be in that barn with that ugly mule, or better yet, you would be in that barn with that ugly mule and I would be in the cabin with Lucy. I know you remember the song I made up about Lucy while on that cattle drive to Ohio. I'll sing it for you Daisy. It goes like this:

Lucy with your long blonde hair and you eyes of blue
Can I touch you?
Lucy you're as juicy as a fresh picked Raspberry
Can I taste you?
Lucy your lips are as moist and the morning dew
Can I kiss you?
Lucy your in my dreams
Will you join me?

I sang that song for you all the way to Ohio. I know you liked it because of the way your ears twitched. Just like they are doing now. Lucy is a real lady but she likes the city life and you know Daisy, I'm just 100% country and could never live in the city.

Lucy has never showed me the attention she shows you. The city is fine to go get a beer, but when my thirst is quenched it's time for the country again. I can only stand so much of those city folks.

Lucy on the other hand, fits anywhere she wants to be, city, country, even in the mountains, she is just that kind of a girl. If she didn't talk so much about the big house in the city that is her dream, I just might have asked if I could court her. No way will I get stuck in a city for a pretty face. It would just go sour and I know that. Why mess up two peoples life, and the kids they have. Daisy, the girl I settle down with and marry, better like living in the country. The city is just for visiting.

I'm so glad you like lessening to me talk Daisy. I work out a lot of problems just talking out loud about them. People say if you talk out loud to yourself it means your crazy. That's why I talk to you Daisy; I don't want people thinking I'm crazy. We better pick up the pace Daisy or it might soon be the death of me. That posse is in the valley just the other side of that ridge."

Bart is quite a charter. I believe he could get an academy award for the performance he is giving. You can't help but like him. He's so sweet, not jumping into Lucy's life, knowing what her dreams are. Bart knows you don't change people and expect them to be happy about it. If you marry, you must have a lot in common or you won't last. He wouldn't hurt Lucy like that.

Bart said, "You know Daisy, you don't have to marry every pretty girl you have a date with. You only marry the one that has the same dreams you have about life. When dating, you let that person know that if your dreams are different, things will just have to be simple with no attachments in the long run. You just enjoy each other's company for the time you are together, than you both move on. That's how it will be with Lucy and me. Simple enjoyment of whatever time we spend together, than we will both move on and make a life for ourselves. I just hope mine doesn't end at the end of a rope.

Daisy, do you remember that time when Lucy and me went panning for gold and we had a picnic in the open air on a quilt she made by hand? It was full of different colors that were from dresses she had worn since she was a little girl. It had a lot of her history in it and we talked about every piece of material in it. For lunch Lucy had cooked fried chicken and biscuit's. She had fresh sliced tomatos out of her garden with just a little salt for flavor. For desert she had fresh raspberries that she gathered out of the woods. Lucy sure does things like a country girl, why do you think she wants to be a city slicker? Lucy even brought oats and sugar cubs for you and that mule of hers. She seemed to be more excited about you being there with us than she was about me. She didn't even say anything to you when you stepped on her hand made quilt while nudging her for another sugar cube. She just kissed you on the nose and said, 'Isn't that the curettes thing?' Yes Daisy, you stole Lucy's heart the moment she laid eyes on you. You know, she never kissed me.

The most fun I had while staying with Lucy was when we went to the redo. It was a perfect evening weather wise. Those cowboys were riding some real strong bucking broncos. Most didn't even last five seconds, but you could see in their eyes that it was a very exciting five seconds. The bull riders were having an even tougher time staying on those vicious bucking bulls. One poor guy got picked up by a horn and thrown over the fence. He broke a leg and an arm. This sport is not for the faint of heart. Most bull riders break several bones before they finally give up on ridding bulls. It just gets into their blood. You know Daisy, I'm glad we do the barrel racing; it's a lot safer. The guys ridding the bulls and breaking their bones will be hurting in their old age. You know those injuries haunt you when your old every day. I don't like pain so we will stick to barrel racing.

You know Daisy, you are very good at cutting quick corners and that is why we won the competition that night. You were light on your hoofs and fast as the wind. It was like we were floating around those barrels. We picked up some pocket change and brought Lucy a pink bonnet with a matching purse. She got so excited she gave both of us a hug around the neck. It felt real nice. She sure was pretty that Sunday all dressed up for church in that pink bonnet. It matched her cheeks and lips. She looked real nice that day. When she asked if she could ride you to church, I couldn't say no. Lucy is the only person to have ever ridden you other than myself. You two sure looked nice that day. If the posse finds me at Lucy's cabin, I'm going to give you to her. If they find me I think I'm a dead man.

Talking to you Daisy helps to keep that awful thought out of my mind. I don't cherish the thought of dieing for what I thought was the right thing to do. It all happened so fast, I just reacted. Anyway, if they do catch me, Lucy will take good care of you if we make it to the cabin."

Bart wonders if Lucy will still welcome him if she finds out that he killed a man? Will she believe the story if he tells her what happened? Will she see a wanted poster and turn him in? Bart wants to tell her but fears she will ask him to leave. He will just have to take that chance. He would rather leave than feel she would turn him into the authorities.

Bart's only a few miles away from Lucy's house now and its time to cover all tracks left by his horse. Bart knows they are tracking his prints because they cannot see him. He ties a rope to Daisy's saddle, and a log on the end of the rope so they can drag it sideways to cover his tracks. Bart's horse Daisy can pull this log if Bart is not on her back. Bart leads his horse through the valley and when it's time to go up the side of the mountain he cuts the log lose. The rest of the way is rocks so no tracks will be found.

When he gets to Lucy's cabin she is not there. She pans for gold around this time because the sun hit's it just right and it's easier to find the gold flakes. She will be back in an hour or so. Bart takes the saddle off his horse and takes her to the barn. Lucy is ridding her mule and there is enough hay for both of them tonight, so Bart feeds and waters Daisy. When Lucy comes up the path she sees Bart sitting on the steps in front of her door. She jumps off her mule and runs to see him. As Bart stands up, Lucy grabs him around the neck with her arms and hugs him tight. "I've missed you so much," Lucy said.

This is a good sign. A friendly face for now, time will tell. Bart decides to not tell Lucy about the posse tonight, he just wants a good hot meal and a bath. He will deal with this in the morning. As nighttime comes crashing in a light rain shower began to fall from the heavens. Bart always sleeps well when it rains, and he desperately needs a good night sleep. Lucy lightly brushed Bart's hair from his eyes. The rain now dripping off the roof of the cabin is like a lullaby, a soothing song intended to lull a child to sleep, and right now Bart is weak as a baby as he drifts into a deep slumber.

The morning sun creeps up the side of the mountain creating a luminous landscape of rock, trees and snow capped peaks. The view is breathtaking and the air is sweet with the scent of fresh rain. Lucy is cooking hot cakes with honey and a couple of over easy fresh eggs. Just what Bart needed to start the day with, an energy meal to build his strength back with for the day ahead? Lucy brought him a cup of hot coffee and Bart just sat on the edge of the bed sipping the coffee until breakfast was ready.

Lucy is beyond excited, she is in an exultant mood, marked by great joy and jubilation, that Bart is in her house. After breakfast Lucy brought a clear bottle filled with flakes of gold to the table. She showed this to Bart and said, "There is enough gold in this bottle to buy half the mountain I got it out of." Bart started to say something, but Lucy put two fingers over his mouth and said, "Let me finish. When I first started gathering gold out of the streams of this mountain, I had plans of buying a large home in town, and setting myself up for financial freedom for the rest of my life. This little cabin was just a stepping-stone to what I thought was the life I wanted. Now all I want is the beautiful view of that mountain, this cabin with a couple of more rooms, my mule, chickens, pigs and cows. Oh yes, and I want to buy the side of that mountain. I want to start a family with a husband and have a cabin full of children. You know Bart that I have feelings for you and your not getting any younger. If you could settle down for a couple of months and stay with me to see if you can develop feelings for me, maybe we could share a life together." Bart just sat with his jaw dropped, and his eyes wide open in amazement. He couldn't have a more perfect situation.

Bart said, "Lucy there is something I must tell you about myself." Lucy put her fingers over Bart's mouth once again and said, "Your past is your past. I want to start our life from this moment forward. Please just give it a while and if you need to move on that will be fine. Just give it a couple of months."

Things couldn't be working out better for Bart. This is a perfect hideout until he can find out what is being said about the shoot-out in the saloon. You just never know what people will say when it's their friend that's involved. Somehow Bart needs to find out what that posse thinks he's done. Are they wanting to take him in alive or is dead just as good. Will Bart be able to go into town and read what the Wanted Poster says about him? Will someone recognize him? What will Lucy think if she sees the Wanted Poster with Bart's face on it? Will she turn him in for the reward? Bart has all these situations to deal with, and it's clouding his mind.

Lucy and Bart set out to go panning for gold up the side of

the mountain. Lucy leads with her mule and Bart followed with his palomino horse, Daisy. His palomino horse has a golden coat with a white and cream-colored mane and tail. As pretty a horse as I've ever seen. They grew up together and can read each other's moves. You can see that in the movie. It's unspoken but the eye knows their bond. Occasionally Daisy turns her head to look at Bart and you can see they are pals. Lucy's mule seems to be task oriented. Not a lot of personality.

As they reach their destination Lucy turns and says, "This little stream has a pot of gold just waiting to be scooped up. We need to walk the rest of the way. You can tie Daisy under that tree. Here's your pan. Just scoop up some sand and roll it around until you find some gold flakes. Don't let fools gold fool you. It is hard and gold is soft. This stream has a vein of gold somewhere; I just haven't found it yet. When I do find it, I'll strike a claim."

Bart began panning and filled his little vile with gold flakes in no time at all. Lucy talked the whole time she was panning. Lucy said, "You know Bart that gold is the only mineral that never changes, no matter what we do to it. Gold is rare and is conductive to produce electricity. I'm not trying to build you into something your not, I know you love driving cattle, but I think you can develop a passion for panning gold. With gold you can buy all the cattle you want, and drive them to the marketplace. The difference would be instead of taking orders you would be giving them." Lucy looked at Bart with a big smile on her face, and Bart returned the look with a full set of teeth showing. Looks like they are on the same sheet of music. Lucy said, "We need to find lots of gold because it takes lot's of acres of land to feed cattle, the land here is so rocky and grass needs dirt to grow. I figure we need 300 acres for every 100 cattle. There's plenty of water in the streams so we won't have to dig ponds for them. The cattle can pretty much take care of themselves."

They both found enough gold to fill their vile in a short amount of time. Lucy decided it is time to go back to the cabin. Lucy needed supplies from town and asked Bart to accompany her. He just wanted to hang out and enjoy the luxury of the cabin and give Daisy a good brush down. Lucy asked if he wanted anything and he said, "Some oats for Daisy," then Lucy headed for town. When she got there the posse was in the saloon asking questions about a man on the Wanted Posters and they were sticking posters up all over town. Lucy was in the supply store when she seen one of the posters. She took it down and put it in her pocket. When she returned to the cabin she showed it to Bart and asked if he had a twin brother. Bart said, "I tried to tell you and you put your hand over my mouth and said you did not want to know anything about my past. I planned to tell you eventually before I asked you to marry me. Just not while you are so happy to see me." Lucy said, "What happened that it takes twenty men to find you. You are worth a lot of money according to this Wanted Poster, $500 to be exact."

Bart said, "Sit down Lucy and I will explain what happened." When Bart finished explaining everything, Lucy suggested that she go to New Mexico to the little town where all this happened, and find out if Bart can get a fair trail. Lucy said, "If I'm going to marry you I need to get to the bottom of things. I'm going to take a stagecoach to that little town and talk to the bar maid that got shot. Together we will get this thing taken care of. I need to know if you can get a fair trail, if not, you will just have to live in these mountains away from everyone who may hurt you."

When Lucy got to the town she started asking questions about whom all seen what happened in the gunfight. There are two different stories being told. One by the friends of the cigar chewing man that Bart put a bullet in and another by the bar maid who got shot in the shoulder. Lucy paid the bar maid a visit and got the real story. She knows the real story is that Bart kicked the guns out of the two shooters hands so they could not hurt anyone else, and that the cigar chewing man was about to shoot two unarmed men, when Bart killed him. The bar maid told the same exact story.

Lucy asked the bar maid if she would tell the wife of the cigar chewing man, how things really came down. She told the bar maid that a crazed posse is in pursuit of this innocent man and they may kill him on site. The bar maid agreed to talk to the widow. She just didn't believe that a woman with such status would believe her husband could possible do such a thing. With Lucy's encouragement, the bar maid got the courage to do what is right. It would be damaging to the family's image to know that her husband would shoot an unarmed man, so the widow requested that the bar maid bring two witness to verify her story and she would talk to the sheriff. The bar maid had no trouble finding other witness who were happy to get rid of the guilt they were carrying around with them. It's hard to go up against powerful people especially when they have helped so many people in the town to have jobs to feed their families. The widow will just have to accept her husband's death for what it is and take the Wanted Posters down before an innocent man dies. The widow went to the sheriff and requested he listen to the stories being told to her. Together they decided to declare the man on the Wanted Poster innocent. The posters were removed and the sheriff wired the posse in Padosa, Colorado to take down the Wanted Posters, and return to New Mexico.

The movie ended with Lucy and Bart panning for gold with their six children right in the stream with them. They added eight rooms onto the cabin with an upstairs play room for the kids. After a day of panning for gold, Bart was getting ready for a cattle drive. He had 500 head rounded up and told the hired help, "You know what to do, lets get these cattle to Kansas." With that the story ended.

I see why it has a four star ratting now. The bang-bang shoot um up for the guys, the love story for the girls and the clean language for the kids. There was something for everyone, a real family movie. They just don't make them like this anymore.

It's intermission time now before the next movie starts. That's what is so good about outdoor movie; you get three movies for the price of just one. Everyone got out of the cars to stretch and get some refreshments. Popcorn sounds good with a bottle of water. Each couple got large popcorns to share with each other. We all really liked Zack's taste in movies. It is one of the best movies I've seen in a long time. The scenery was beautiful, and I wanted to go panning for gold in Colorado now. It looked like a lot of fun.

The next movie was about Aliens who came out of the black hole in the Universe. Humans would chase them with their futuristic spacecrafts, but we would not enter the black hole. We didn't know if we could make it out. We might get lost. There are no stars or moons in the black hole and no one likes being lost. With the moons and stars you can navigate by their locations and land exactly where you want to be. This movie was taking place in the year 2050. The Aliens look and talk just like humans except for one major difference, they didn't have belly buttons. You see they were created, not born. Anyway, some were very cute. The Aliens would abduct humans and take them into the black hole, and the humans were never seen again. To get the humans back before the Aliens entered the black hole, we would have a sky race and if we got close enough to their spacecraft we would beam out an invisible bubble, which surrounded their spacecraft and rendered it immobile. The Aliens would then turn over the humans and we would arrest the Aliens and put them in a space module prison.

This movie had a two star ratting but I would give it a two and a half stars. Some of the guys had really good lines when picking up the humans. My favorite line that they used is, 'Would you like to go to a party, you would be the Bell of the Ball, no one there can hold a candle to you, you're so smashingly good looking.' Stroking the ego always works on airheads.

After the Alien movie we decided to leave. There is a third movie but we all agreed to pass on it. It's ratting is a one and a half stars. Will just catch it on television at a later date.

This was a lot of fun, double dating at a drive-in movie. I like being with my friends and sharing a good time. We will have to do this again sometime; right now I just want to go to sleep.

Chapter 2
Sara

BreAnna called early in the morning and invited me to go with her for a pancake at the Flat Jack City restaurant where Sara is working. It sounded like a great idea. Blue berry pancakes are one of my weaknesses. Plus, blue berries give me a lot of energy, which I will need later in the day for soccer practice.

When we walked into the restaurant, Sara was talking to a very handsome man who was sitting at a table by himself. When Sara caught a glimpse of us out of the corner of her eye, a big smile came across her face and she motioned for us to join her. As we were walking towards her she said, "Hi you two, I want you to meet a friend of mine, Nick this is Chelsea and this is BreAnna." Nick nodded his head to acknowledge our existence, glanced at his watch and said, "I really must be going." He left a $5 bill on the table for a $1 dollar cup of coffee. This seemed a little strange.

Sara walked Nick to the door and we seated ourselves at the table. BreAnna looked at me and said, "A very expensive cup of coffee." I nodded in complete agreement. When Sara came back to the table she said, "I don't know what the hurry was, normally, Nick, has a muffin with his coffee. Oh well, what are you two up to." I said, "We just thought we would have some breakfast and watch you work for a while.

If your not busy you could watch us eat." I gave a little giggle so she would know I was only having fun with her. Sara said, "Actually it's time for me to take a break so I'll just have breakfast with you. Chelsea, I know you will want the blue berry pancakes, that's what I'm having also, what about you BreAnna." "I think the English-Muffin with; black currant jelly, is all I need." Sara said, "I'm buying. Be back in a jiff."

Sara seemed super excited about seeing us and that now we are knowing how good looking Nick is with his shinny new red Corvette, she is beaming. I must say, he is quite a package, that is, to look at. He certainly is lacking in the matters department. He wanted nothing to do with Sara's friends. It was clear to us.

Sara first brought out the blue berry pancakes and English-Muffin with black current jelly, and than she came back with our drinks. We could see that Sara is a very good waitress. She can carry the food with the greatest balance ever.

"I'm so glad you two came to see me, we don't get to see each other work. Chelsea, I've been meaning to come see you at the mall so you could help me pick out a sundress, you do have sun dresses at the shop you work at don't you? Nick asked me to ware a dress when I meet him at the movie next week," Sara said. "Yes we have all kinds of dresses and shoes and handbags and even pearl necklaces. You will love the little shop I work in. See this pinky-ring, it was only $20 dollars. That's a real pearl. Pearl's are made from a tiny grain of sand inside an oyster on the coastal marine water. It takes years for that piece of sand to become a pearl. I plan to name my first girl Pearl. I think it's a lovely name," I said. "Your first girl, how many do you plan to have," BreAnna said. "At least two, the other girl will be named Turquoise, it also is a precious stone, made from a blue-green mineral of aluminum and copper. When polished this gemstone becomes a brilliant bluish green. Turquoise is my favorite color and the name has a nice ring to it. I love all the names of stones such as Ruby, Diamond, Pebble, Garnet and Jade. All of these are great names. If I have seven children and all are girls, I will use all those names," I said.

"What do you two think about Nick? Is he as handsome as I said he was?" said Sara. "He's very handsome, but he was in a hurry to leave. We didn't get a chance to talk to him," BreAnna said.

Sara changed the subject immediately it was as if she did not want to address the fact that Nick did not want anything to do with her friends. Also he looks older than any 18 years old. He looks to be in his twenties. Why can't Sara see this fact of life? I'm concerned about the fact that Nick nearly runs away when Sara's friends enter the picture. Something just doesn't feel right with this situation.

After we finished breakfast Sara gave us a hug and she went back to taking orders and serving customers coffee. We watched her work for a while and left her a good tip. She came by the table and said, "You don't need to tip me you are my friends." We left the tip anyway and waved good-by as we went out the door.

For the next three hours we went skating. This is one of my favorite ways to build strength in my legs. It's a lot of fun so you don't realize all the work you are doing, but you feel the strength in your body that is the results of roller-skating. The other way we, by we, I mean the Headbangers, build strength in our legs is by running up a hill near the soccer field. That is a real workout. My legs have grown muscles since I started running up and down that hill.

Skating helps with our balance as well as building our endurance. We skate backwards which impacts muscles we didn't even know we had. You can feel it pull the muscles from your heel all the way to your neck. It is amazing what the body can do if proper training is applied.

After the skating workout we headed for the soccer

field for practice. The Headbangers decided to meet thirty minutes early to practice our new move. Little did we know that coach Ross always goes to practice early, for some one on one coaching, for players who are having a difficult time mastering certain moves. Coach Ross and the two players he was coaching stopped what they were doing and just watched what the Headbangers were doing.

After watching for a while, coach Ross asked if the two players could join the Headbangers to learn the move we were perfecting. "Of course, anything we can do to improve the team and inspire others would be a badge of honor for the Headbangers," BreAnna said.

The two girls joined us and the first thing BreAnna did was talk to them, "The thing most important in this move is situation awareness, know your surroundings. You must strike the ball with the side of your foot at the exact moment that the players think the ball will be going in the opposite direction. Strike the ball to your teammate, they will header the ball, into the net. We throw our opponents off with this move by starting it on our knee, than the side of our foot like this, than to a teammate high enough for the header hit, do you follow." The girls nodded their heads in acknowledgement.

These two girls caught on fast and when the rest of the team arrived for practice, coach Ross split us up into teams and this move was perfected by the time practice was over. As the Headbangers were walking to their cars, Angela said, "That was inspirational. Coach Ross just took that move and made it part of the teams program." Angela raised her hand for a high five and we all responded.

This day took a lot of energy out of me and when I got home I poured myself a large glass of tea and went out on the backyard patio to just lay down on a lounge chair and rest. I must have fallen asleep because the next thing I knew Bam was sniffing my hair and woke me up. I said, "Hey girl what are you doing? You woke me up. Do you need some attention or are you hungry? I miss you to."

Bam is either getting fat or she has a baby bump in her belly. I wonder if it will be a male or female, or if it will be as friendly as Bam herself. I rubbed Bam on her belly and she looked at me with pride in her eyes. Mom walked out the door and called out to me, "I'm out here in the backyard," I said. Mom said, "I didn't see you. Would you like some fried chicken for dinner? If you would please pick a couple of fresh tomato's, with a hand full of okra out of the garden I will prepare them for a meal. I'll boil them together with a little salt and pepper. We can get everything ready before your dad gets home."

That sounds so good. I have worked up quite an appetite today. Bam followed me to the garden and I threw her a little salad. She is very appreciative when she gets a juice ripe tomato. She always nudges my arm after eating a tomato, it is as if she is saying 'I want more', or 'Thank you,' which ever it is, she always wiggles her ears and tail. While walking towards the house I gave her another tomato and said, "This one is for baby Bam."

Dad walked in the door right as the salad hit the table. "I'm excited to see you dad, I want to tell you and mom that coach Ross adopted the new move that the Headbangers have been practicing for the past week. He had the whole team practice it for the entire practice session," I said. "That's great! Sounds to me like this could to be a very interesting season. I'm happy for you and your friends," dad said. With that came a group hug and some finger licking good chicken.

Sara called right before I went to bed to get the hours that I would be working for the week. Her big date was coming up soon and she wanted to be looking good. We talked about the crush she is developing on Nick and she let me know how shy he is and that when the time is right, he will meet all her friends. Right now they are getting to know each other better. She talked about how she sees him every morning at 6:00am on the dot. He spends an hour sipping coffee and watching her work. She talked about how she can feel his eyes on her every move.

Personally he gives me the creeps. The more Sara tells me about him the more he creeps me out. He sounds like a stalker, only where the person being stalked is allowing it.

Sara must have modeled twelve different sundresses before she choose a white, eye lit dress with thin straps. If I must say so myself she does look stunting in this very clean looking sundress. The dress has an eloquence to it that makes Sara look much older than seventeen. The handbag Sara chose was a soft white leather with red trim. The shoes were a solid red, but they were made with only thin pieces of red leather that matched the trim on her purse. The excitement in her voice made me happy for her, but at the same time, this guy Nick just didn't feel right for Sara to me. Sara said, "It's a shame that Nick is not picking me up in his red Corvette, my outfit would match it perfect." When Sara said that, it reminded me of what I don't like about Nick. What kind of guy wants to meet you at a movie instead of picking you up from your home? The warning bells went off in my head once again.

Angela dropped by the dress shop, knowing Sara was going to be trying on dresses for her big day at the movies with Nick. Angela invited us to go rock climbing later in the day. She let us know the guys, Brad, Kyle, Zack, and Jake would be there. Angela said, " Rock climbing will be the exercise that will build strength in our legs and arms, that should help us on the soccer field." Sara said, "Yes, you can count on me being there."

When we arrived, BreAnna called out, "Over here, glad to see you two could make it. Angela is on her way, she just called my cell phone." As Sara and I neared the wall we looked up and saw the guys halfway up the rock wall. This did not look like an easy task. I believe a lot of muscles are being flexed as they reach for the piece of rock to push on to the top of the wall. BreAnna said, "When they get down we will show them how to climb like we have done it all our lives. Climbing the hills like we already do, has given us the strength we need to make it to the top."

Kyle slipped, and lost his footing, thank goodness he is tied off with a rope and won't fall. All the other guys are nearing the top of the wall, Kyle is still only half way up the wall, it's like he froze in place and was not able to keep his footing. Suddenly Kyle got his grip and started back up the wall. The other guys were on their way back down but Kyle was determined to make it to the top. Sara said, "That's what I like about Kyle, he just doesn't give up, that's right, he is no quitter." A big smile came across Sara's face as she took pride in the fact that Kyle was determined to make it to the top. Kyle is known for his brains, not his muscle mass.

The other guys are making their way back down. As they pass Kyle, we could hear them saying, "Don't give up buddy, we know you can do it. See you at the bottom." It looks like coming down the rock wall is a lot easier than going up. Kyle is finally to the top of the wall. He yells out, "I made it." The guys stopped in their tracks, looked up at Kyle and yelled back, "Way to go, we knew you could make it to the top." All of us girls were clapping our hands chanting, "Go Kyle, go Kyle, go Kyle."

When all the guys got back down to earth, Kyle started talking about what happened to him on the rock wall. He said, "I froze, totally rendered immobile, incapable of any movements, for a rather long moment. Thoughts were going through my head, like, my friends are going to have to call the fire department to rescue me. The fire department will have to put a ladder up the rock wall and a fireman will have to pry my hands lose to get me off this wall. Nothing like that has ever happened to me before."

Sara put her arm around Kyle's waist and said, " It's called a fear of heights. It happens to a lot of people. You went to the top so maybe you have conquered your fears." "What I did was, just not look down to the bottom of the rock wall. I kept my eyes on the target, the top of the rock wall. When I started going down, my eyes stayed on the top of the wall. If I were to look down, I think I might have froze up again," Kyle said.

It's time for the Headbangers to climb the rock wall now. We all took note of what happened to Kyle, I'm certain we will be looking at the top of the rock wall all the way up and all the way down. This is very changeling on the fingers and our legs will be getting the workout of a lifetime. My body is being stretched beyond anything I have experienced in my life. My muscles are burning but the thrill of making it to the top blocks the pain. BreAnna called out, "Don't get weak on me girls, were almost to the top." She must be feeling her muscles burning just like I do or she would not have said that.

BreAnna was the first to reach the top and called out to us, "I won't start back down until all four of us has reached the top." One by one we made it to the top of this rock wall. It was not an easy task, but very exciting. We rejoiced as we began our decent back to earth. It's much easier going down this rock wall than it was going up it.

Kyle cut a straw into eight pieces, with only one being short. Zack winded up being the one holding the short straw. His new word is repercussion and the meaning is, an indirect effect, influence or result created by an action or event. Zack's example goes like this, "If you pollute your mind with foul words or foul thoughts, eventually they become part of your persona, the repercussion of your actions will be damaging. It's very much like what you put into your body by what you eat. If you pollute your body with drugs, white flour, sugar, corn syrup and cameral colored soft drinks, the repercussions are that your cells cannot provide your body with the nutrition needed to live a healthy life.

The repercussion is your blood cells are toxic. The mind and body determine your future happiness. You are the one's who choose to make your mind and body unfit. If you poison your mind and body the repercussion is injury, illness, or early death."

"Well put Zack," said Jake. "You sound just like Chelsea," Kyle said, "That could be because I spend so much time around her. I've been preparing for when I would draw the short straw, that's why it did not take any time for me to give examples of how to use the word repercussion," Zack said. "I'm proud to have such an influence on you Zack, I hope I'm contagious and this mindset spreads," I said. "Don't worry Chelsea, you have already reached everyone at this table," Angela said.

That night, I drew a hot bath with two cups of Epson Salt to help sooth my aching muscles. Afterwards, I rubbed my legs with alcohol to help prevent any muscles from stiffing up. Rock climbing is going to be one of my fun way's to stay in good shape from now on.

Sara's big date, or big meeting at the movies, whatever you want to call it, is taking place today. Sara asked if she could stay the night with me after the movie, and I was impressed that she wanted to share this day with me. It's always nice to share exciting times with a friend. Sara is unaware that Nick gives me the creeps. Before I tell her about my feelings, Nick will have to validate those feelings with his actions.

Sara called much sooner than I expected. This date, or whatever she wants to call it, only lasted for two hours. No longer than the movie itself. When Sara pulled into my driveway, I went out on the front poach to greet her. Sara looked lovely. Her hair is up on her head with streamers lightly brushing her neck. The dress, shoes and bag are stunting. As she nears my front door she spins in a circle with her arms above her head like a ballerina dancer. Sara is grinning from ear to ear. As she walked into the house she said, "Let go to the bench by the pond, the evening is cool and I want to be in the outdoors. Do you mind if I pour myself a glass of lemon aid." "Let me get some ice and I'll pour it for you," I said.

As we walked to the pond Bam came up behind us. Sara gave her a hug around her neck and scratched behind her ear. As we set down on the bench and gazed upon the cool spring fed pond, Sara began telling me the details of her first date with Nick. Sara said, "Nick gave me instructions to enter the theater through the left door and count thirty seats down, and he would be there. Our first date would be Dutch treat, which does not bother me since he tips me at my job every day. Anyway, when I sat down he told me I looked lovely. That just filled my heart with joy. When the movie started, Nick put his arm around my neck and gave me a hug and kiss on the ear. The movie was sexual by nature and a bit racy, boarding on risqué in my books. Anyway, Nick whispered in my ear that I was much prettier than the female star in the movie, than he kissed my ear again. As time went on Nick had an asthma attack or something. His breathing became labored, like he had a chest constriction. I asked him if he was okay, and suddenly he caught his breath and was normal. Near the end of the movie, Nick put his hand on my knee and began to push my dress up and I had to stop him. Nick told me he could not help himself he just wanted to touch me.

After the movie was over, Nick said he wanted me to go ahead and leave, that he was going to just sit and enjoy the moment. I waited across the street in the little ice cream shop to watch him leave. When Nick came out of the theater, he was looking left to right as if he was looking for me. Than, he got into his red Corvette and left. He told me that until I'm eighteen, he would like things this way to help keep it simple and from getting out of hand. I think it is a good idea because I really like being around him. Besides I will be eighteen soon anyway."

Sara must be blinded by Nicks good looks, and shinny red Corvette, to not see something is not right about this whole scenario. I refuse to let myself wake her up to this guy Nick, while she is so happy and pretty in her new outfit with her hair fixed so cute. I've never seen Sara look so pretty. I said, "Sara, how about I get dressed up in my Sunday best and we go out to eat, just the two of us. Let's go somewhere nice, a fancy restaurant." "Sounds great to me, how about a place where we can get fish, down by Lake Tenkiller," Sara said. I nodded my head in agreement and we headed back towards the house. I turned on my computer so Sara could entertain herself with internet access. After my shower, thoughts were going through my head about different ways to fix my hair. I want to try something different, kind of like the way Sara has her hair on top of her head with some curls. I heated up my curling iron and went to work on this artistic design for my hair. I'm having fun with this and Sara offered to help. We had a great time getting ready for the evening. Sometimes getting ready to go somewhere is as much fun as the place you go to.

As we pulled up to Lake Tenkiller the view was breathtaking. The sun was bringing out the blue and green color that only nature can create. Every time I see this lake it warms my heart. It is one of God's perfect creations.

The restaurant has a waiting line, that always means good food. When we did get seated it was in a booth overlooking the lake. Perfect to top off a great evening.

The fish has a nice white color and is light and flaky. It melts in my mouth with each bite. The broccoli, yellow corn, and cauliflower have just enough crunch that the flavor exploded with each bite. The cornbread muffins are filled with blueberries and onions. For desert we ordered a piece of pineapple upside down cake. It was a perfect meal, a perfect view, and a perfect evening, to top off Sara's day.

On the way home, Sara thanked me for suggesting we

entertain ourselves, since she was all dressed up with no where to go, but a dark movie where people only get a glance of her new outfit. When a person goes through all the work to get gussy up, they want to share their look with others. Sara does look stunting. I'm looking pretty good myself. We get a lot of looks and a couple of nods. It's like we put on our own little fashion show. It was fun.

The next day Angela came by to talk to me about this Nick guy. Sara had called Angela to tell her all about her movie date with Nick. Angela also got bad vibes while Sara told her story about the date. "There is just something not right about this guy Nick not wanting to be seen in public. At the restaurant he sits in the back of the building, so not to be noticed by anyone. He is hiding something. A red flag went up when Sara told me she met him at the movie and after the movie, he stayed in the theater and had Sara leave by herself. He does not want to be seen with Sara. I think Brad needs to investigate this guy. Do you know that Sara doesn't even know Nick's last name? He told her when she turns eighteen he will tell her his full name. There is something wrong with that also. I talked with Brad about this situation and he is going to do some investigating. Brad gets a big kick out of getting to the bottom of a situation that doesn't smell right. You know that is why he wants to be a DEA agent when he gets out of school. Tomorrow Brad is going to follow Nick around, only because he also feels that Sara could get hurt. Brad believes in prevention, nip bad situations in the bud before they blossom into disaster," Angela said. "That sounds like a great idea. I wanted to tell Sara to snap out of this daze that Nick has her in, but she seems so taken by him that I think she would resent me saying anything. I just couldn't do it while she was so excited about the whole Dutch date. If Brad finds out anything, that would be the time to tell her. Hard evidence is what we need. Nick being older than Sara is not a crime. We could all just be overreacting to this situation because he doesn't want to be around us," I said.

It was two days before Brad completed his investigation of just who Nick is, but now we are fixing to find out. Angela called to see if her and Brad could come by to talk. I fixed a picture of lemonade and filled three glasses with ice. When Angela and Brad arrived we went on the back patio with our lemonade drinks in hand. Brad said, "Chelsea, I have some information on Nick Yates. I found out his last name when I followed him to church and seen him talking to a man for a lengthy amount of time. After he left I approached this man and told him I had known Nicks first name but did not know his last name and could he tell me. This man told me that Nick's last name is Yates and his wife's name is Janet. They are expecting a baby next month according to this man's statement. He said that Janet has been confined to bed rest until the baby is born and that is why she could not attend services. Nick and his wife live two counties away, approximately 50 miles from here. Nick is 20 years old, not 18 years old like he told Sara. His parents gave him a job as foreman of their construction company and bought him the red Corvette that he drives. He is here in Tahlequah overseeing the new building going up on the other side of town. All he does is watch the other guys work. He's probably never even had a hammer in his hand. This Nick is anything but what Sara thinks he is."

"This is awful. How are we going to tell Sara that Nick is not the man he portrayed himself to be? Who is going to break her heart with the bad news," I said. "No one is going to tell her, that is no friend is going to tell her. I've talked to Zack and we are going to the construction site to pay Nick a visit. We are going to give him a choice to tell Sara, himself, that he is married, or we will be going to the town where he lives, and tell the preacher where he goes to church about his activities in Tahlequah with a seventeen year old girl who knows nothing about him being married. We think he will make the right choice," Brad said.

"This whole thing with Nick is just wrong. It hurts me that she will have to go through this. I hope that she never finds out that we intervened in her relationship with Nick. Can we be sure he won't tell Sara we talked to him," I said. "To begin with, as far as Nick knows, only myself and Zack will be aware of the situation. If he mentions our names to Sara, we may have to mention Sara's name to his parents that gave him his job. I don't think he would want to risk them taking away his toy, the red Corvette," Brad said.

"That Nick is such a scumbag, his wife is having a baby and is confined to bed rest, while he is making moves on a seventeen year old girl. That is disgraceful, and shame is his middle name," Angela said.

Nick paid Sara a visit three days later, and that is the last any of us ever seen or heard from him. After that last visit Sara never spoke the name Nick again. She seemed down for a couple of weeks, but snapped back rather quickly. Sara was in ah of Nick's looks and the nice car that he drove was just exciting to her. I never heard her say how much she cared about Nick. This is something certain girls just go through. The old saying 'all that glitters is not gold' applies to this situation. The glamour of a shining new red Corvette, and who gets a $5 dollar tip for a muffin and cup of coffee. On top of all that Nick is very handsome, and more experienced, seeing how he is 20 years old. I just figure he is going through something in life right now himself. His wife is confined to bed rest because of her difficult pregnancy and Nick is in need of attention. When a person is self-absorbed, as I see Nick being, it is a perfect time for the Devil to step in and take control of one's life. What Nick was doing with Sara is evil. If Nick's wife ever knew about what he was doing with Sara, it would change their relationship forever. They would probably wind up as a statistic of the divorce numbers that are completely out of control.

This situation hopefully brought Nick back to reality before he caused great harm to a lot of people. Unlike Angela, who thinks Nick is a scumbag, I think the devil has temped him, after all he does go to church, and he is starting a family by marrying the girl he loves. To me he looks like someone who is trying to do the right thing in life but got side tracked by circumstances. Hopefully this is a one-time thing that Brad and Zack stopped before it ruined a marriage. I'm hoping that Nick is a good guy that did a bad thing, and got caught. It might be just a one-time thing that will never happen again. I like to see the best in people. Everyone makes mistake in life, hopefully they learn from their mistakes.

Chapter 3

Noodling

The noodling contest tomorrow will have a $500 prize for whoever pulls out the biggest catfish, in a five hour period. Zack has asked Brad to be his partner, to make sure the winning catfish doesn't drowned him before he gets the fish on land. Noodling alone can be very dangerous because anything can happen.

The catfish are very strong, and they can clamp down on your arm with their mouth and they don't let go. If a noodler gets a hold of a catfish that is stronger than him or her, they could drown, yes a catfish can kill a human, by submerging and suffocating a person in the water. If the fish were to clamp down on the arm and swim to the bottom of the lake or river, a person could drown before the fish lets go. These fish can weigh well over 60 pounds and they are in their element. Fish are stronger pound for pound in the water than people are.

I'm glad Zack asked Brad to be his partner in this noodling contest. Brad is very strong and he would break the catfishes jaw if he needed to in order to save Zack's life. I don't think any fish could take both of them down.

Zack invited all of us to witness him win this contest. We packed our lunches and brought chairs and blankets to sit on. Under our clothes we wore swimsuits for an occasional dip to cool us down.

I brought the drinks, bottled water and a picture of tea on ice, in my ice chest. Angela brought carrot sticks and celery sticks. BreAnna brought a throw away camera and promised to get each of us copies. Sara brought sandwiches. The guys, Jake and Kyle, brought baked chips. The other two guys, Zack and Brad, put on the show for the rest of us.

The contest is starting and Zack dove under the water and came up with a ten-pound blue cat with a white belly. I jumped up and said, "That's my favorite kind of catfish. Zack can I have him for supper if you find a bigger one." Zack brought this fish to shore and put him on a stringer, tied the stringer to a tree and threw the fish back in the water. Brad said, "That's amazing, let me try to get one." Zack was explaining with lots of hand instructions to Brad where the fish are hiding. From where we are sitting it looks like the fish are up under some kind of rock at the bottom of the lake.

Brad disappeared under the water, and as we all looked on, suddenly Brad surfaces with what looked like a seven pound green catfish. Brad called out, "Hey Chelsea do you want this one also." Before I could answer Angela said, "That's my fish, I'm cooking him for super." We all laughed at her enthusiasm, and Brad was inspired by her reaction to his noodling ability. Brad put the fish on the stringer and was back in the water with a splash. When Brad surfaced the next time, the catfish looked to weigh four pounds. Angela called out, "He's not much bigger than a minnow, let it go unless you want to use him for bait." We all got a kick out of that.

We are two hours into the contest when Zack brings up a forty-pound blue cat. Everyone raced towards the shoreline to see this fish. This big daddy could make Zack the winner of the contest. He is a beauty of a fish. As Zack put him on a stringer he said, "Guys, this one will feed the whole bunch of us. Your all invited to my house tonight for a fish fry."

Zack was exhausted, drained of all his energy. He must have went under water twenty times looking for this fish. When he found him, the fish put up a good fight. They rolled around in the water like they were both fighting for their life. The fish had his mouth clenched tightly on Zack's arm. His sharp teeth broke the skin and Zack was bleeding on both sides of his arm.

A group of ducks flew over our heads, and it was as if they were clapping their wings for Zack's big catch. They flew so close I felt the wind from their wings on my face.

It was time for lunch, and a break for Zack and Brad. Their skin is wrinkling up like a raisin. They had way too much water, for way to long, on their skin. I threw each of them a towel and said, "This should help."

Zack poured himself a paper cup of tea and filled his plate with carrot sticks and celery. If you are going to be swimming and tackling large fish, you want to eat light. Can't afford any cramps in your legs or arms. That would give the fish a big advantage. Brad on the other hand filled his plate with chips and a sandwich. Brad is more of an observer, making sure the fish doesn't eat Zack or drown him.

Jake and Kyle are analyzing this sport of noodling and believe it to be dangerous. Kyle said, "You know my fingers are very important when playing the piano, what happens if a Beaver is in one of those holes you are putting your hand in." Zack said, "If that Beaver bit's off a finger you better catch him so it can be sowed back on." Everyone got a chuckle out of that answer.

Jake said, "Seriously, aren't you afraid of what is in that murky water or that whole that you are sticking your hand in, there could be a poisonous snake that could kill you." "I'm more afraid of the hundred pound catfish that I just won't be able to say no to. I would have to try to bring him to shore and he could very well have me for lunch." Zack said.

We hung out on shore for an hour eating our lunch and listening to fish stories when Zack said, "Brad we really must get back in that water and look for that hundred pound catfish. He is waiting for me and I'm ready to dance with him." Sara said, "Why don't we all take a half hour and swim for awhile. It's getting hot sitting on this blanket."

With that, we all jumped into the water. Not a lot of swimming because our tummies are full, but a lot of splashing and jumping off the guys shoulders. Jake is having a difficult time holding BreAnna on his shoulders because she is so tall and big boned. I seen Jakes head go under water twice. I'm prepared to save him if necessary.

Zack said, "Enough already, I've got a date with a catfish. Come on Brad, let's go hunting."

This time Zack and Brad went around the bend to hunt fish, I guess they thought we scared them all off with the splashing. The rest of us caught some rays and talked about school starting soon. We make it fun for each other, that way no one will be temped to drop out.

The drop out ratio for sixteen and seventeen year olds is very high. They have the opportunity to be driving a car, holding down a full time job, and even working two jobs. If teens get to choose whether to graduate from high school, or keep working their summer jobs, they may choose to drop out of high school. Big mistake! It's only two more years, and the best two years of all the school they have had so far. You have sports, ROTC, Tech classes to learn a high paying trade, and Prom. These are very exciting events that you can't get back if you drop out. People who drop out of school, later in life have profound regrets for their actions. They don't go to high school reunions because it always says the graduating class of whatever year. They never see their friends from school because they lose contact. They don't have as much in common any more. A person should always look way down the road into the future before deciding to drop out of high school. If they do this, they will decide to stay and graduate, I'm certain of it.

"I'm taking biology this year. It is the science of living organisms and life processes, including the study of structure, functioning, growth, evolution, and distribution of living organisms. I want to learn more about amphibians. I want to learn more about cold-blooded, smooth-skinned vertebrate organisms, like frog, that typically hatches as aquatic larvae that breathe by means of gills and metamorphose to an adult form with air-breathing lungs. Also I'm amazed that they can grow new limbs. That's right, they can lose a leg and grow it back. If scientist can figure out how they grow new legs, someday mankind may be able to do the same, like grow a new arm if they lost it in an accident. This is why you learn to dissect a frog. You get to surgically cut tissue to examine and analyze why they can grow new limbs. To make the class more interesting, why don't you all join me," BreAnna said.

"I'm up for it. If you guys would be so kind as to join me in taking Advanced Government, so we can learn how our government works, and the class will be more fun with you there, after all, we will be voting when we turn eighteen years old. Most young people do not know who their Congressman is or what he stands for. Congress runs our country and it is the most important position in our government other than the Supreme Court. I want all of us to learn how our country works in this Advanced Government class. This is the first year for our school to offer Advanced Government. In the days when my grandparents were in school, this class was called Civics, the branch of political science concerned with civic affairs.

To me there is nothing more important than making an informed decision when a person goes to the polls to vote. Too many Americans have fought for our freedoms and died in battle, for us not to take an interest. We must never forget how this country became the greatest in the world. If we don't protect our country, we will become a third world nation, because of the politicians we elect. To often today politicians seek personal or partisan gain, often by crafty or dishonest means. Americans need to know the background of the person running for office. They need to vote for the persons moral fiber, not the smile on their face or because the person is good looking. We owe that to the people who have died fighting for our country," Jake said.

"That's just what I like about you Jake, you look at the big picture, you are aware that your little world of toys and friends can be shattered if you don't take an interest in the big world around you. The lawmakers we will be electing next year with our vote can make a significant impact on our freedoms. For example, if an elected official wanted to make the sport of noodling against the law because he or she felt sorry for the fish, he or she could put it in a bill with several other issues to be voted on. If the bill passes, than it becomes against the law to go noodling. It would take away this great sport that until today, I never even knew existed. Our good friends, Zack and Brad, could become criminals if they tried to continue doing what they loved, the sport of noodling. You see there are these people who think that fish and chickens are animals when in reality they are not. They have a complete different nervous system. Fish and chickens don't feel pain the same way that dogs and cats do. Fish and chickens do not give live birth, and therefore they are not animals with nervous systems that respond to external stimuli. They are cold-blooded creatures that God put on earth for man to eat and catch any way he can.

We must know the people we are electing into the offices that make changes to take away our freedoms. We must protect any freedoms being attacked because some day it could be something dear to your hearts that is being taken away, and making criminals out of you for doing what you have always done, fishing with a worm on a hook," Sara said.

"I think being a Congressman is in my future. I could protect my friend's sports and make sure my country remains the greatest in the world. I know all of you will help campaign for me. The only way I can reach my political goal is with help from my friends. I don't have thousands of dollars to buy my way into office, so you guys will have to go door to door to spread my message. I think I will run for a local office to get my feet wet and make some friends, when I turn eighteen. I can hold a job as a legislator, one who creates or enacts laws, and go to college at the same time. In the political world you must start early and make friends with like-minded people in order to rise up in the ranks.

When I say like-minded people, I'm talking about someone who is aware of the importance of family values. The importance of their children's first six years of life having a family setting so they can develop mentally, and how that will make them strong.

Right now I see gangs and drugs as being on the rise in our country. Gangs are recruiting our young people and branding them with skin illustrations that represent the gang, which they belong to. Then they have these young people push their illegal drugs. In a gang there is very little room at the top, where it is safe as far as going to prison. Since the youth of our nation is doing the dangerous and dirty work of pushing drugs they get scared from the result of this activity. If one is caught dealing drugs and goes to prison, just who do you think will hire them to work for them, when they get out? A life can be ruined with the scars of prison, because the scars of prison, becomes part of that person.

The majority of gang activity is supported by the sale of illegal drugs. If these drugs were provided to the 10% of our society that is addicted to drugs, just who could the gangs sell to? Their market would dry up. The gangs would lose their finances and with that loss of money, they loss power, and members.

We should have free clinics, medical establishments run by several specialists working together, to help with the counceling for addictions for those who walk through the doors. If society provides a place for these addicts to stay, that means they are off the streets and not breaking into homes looking for money to buy drugs with. It would be like a prison but with only drug addicts in it wanting to get well, and real rehab would be the tool to help them.

The streets in the United States are getting more dangerous all the time. We need to look for answers before we fall from within. If working society is afraid to go out at dark, then we are no longer a free society. We lost our freedom from within because we did nothing but make more prisoners, who when released could not get a job so they went back to the only thing they knew, crime," Kyle said.

Sara stood up and clapped her hands and said, "Bravo, bravo." I thought to myself, it's a shame Kyle doesn't go to our school. He has so many ideas that just might work, and I think everyone should hear what he has to say. When he becomes a Congressman they will hear him. He has my vote.

I don't understand anyone wanting to take drugs that become part of their cells that feeds their bodies. Drugs can stay in our cells long after the high, one gets from them is gone. How can anyone risk the chance of conceiving and their baby's be affected by the drugs they took. Life can be altered forever with the dangerous drugs that are on the streets today.

Teens have all this great natural energy that should be put to good use. We can make our own highs the natural ways by what we think. If we control our thought process, we control our happiness. We live in our minds. Why not just alter our thoughts ourselves instead of putting mind altering dangerous drugs in our bodies. That's how I think things should be.

Brad came around the corner with another catfish that looked to weight around ten pounds. He was hopping and hollering as if he had won the contest. When he seen us he said, "This noodling is such a rush. It is so intense when you are feeling around in the dark water, not knowing what you will be bringing to the top. He may not look like much of a fish next to Zack's 40 pound, monster, but he gave me a thrill of a lifetime. I thank him for that."

Brad gave his fish a kiss on its head and put him on a stringer. It was time to get Zack's, 40-pound fish, to the officials to get him weight. When we got there, we were 15 minutes early and a line had already formed. Looking at the fish in the hands of Zack's competition, I would say most look to be the brother and sisters of Zack's fish. It looks to be a very close competition. We could hear numbers being called out, "37 pounds, 35 pounds, and 39 pounds." The closer we got to the weigh station the more excited Zack became. Zack was emitting his excitement in every direction, and we could all feel it. When the official took Zack's fish and weighted it, he called out "42 pounds." That is the highest number we have heard so far. As Zack walked away from the scales, behind him was a gentleman who had a fish very close in size to Zack's. When the official weighted it, he called out, "45 pounds."

It was a close call but Zack came in second. The prize money was only 50 dollars for second place and Zack said, "Will get them next time." He is still upbeat but no longer emitting the energy from the excitement that first place would bring.

We packed our stuff up and headed for Zack's house. When we arrived the dog Molly started barking. Mr. Hughes came out of the house and headed for the outdoors oversize sink where they clean the game, whatever it may be, and wrap it for the freezer.

The fish are put in a vice to hold the head still and Zack drives a nail in the soft spot of the head of the fish. This is instant death for the fish. Dr. Hughes said to Zack, "She is a beauty, we will have her for the fish fry tonight. Put those eggs in a bucket and I will run them over to the wildlife fish observatory so they can hatch them and put the baby catfish back into the lake." This is really something to see. There must be five pounds of fish eggs in the bucket. BreAnna said, "Can we keep some of them for caviar, we could eat them as a appetizer or a garnish on a cracker?" "It's tradition to return all the eggs back to the water they came from, besides we have enough fish here to fill everyone's belly," said Dr. Hughes.

Zack rolled the pieces of fish in buttermilk and then in dry cornmeal. He had around ten pieces prepared and when the peanut oil was bubbling hot he dropped them into the oil. Mrs. Hughes brought an oversized bowl of cold slaw to the picnic table. I said, "Can I help." Mrs. Hughes said, "Sure, if you could put ice in the glasses and pour the tea it would be a big help. Could one of you bring out the hushpuppies?" BreAnna got up and followed me to the house, she helped put ice in the glasses, I got a big tray to carry them on, and BreAnna grabbed the hushpuppies on the way out. Some of the guys were already in line for the first pieces of fish. The smell filled the air and Jake was the first to bite into the forty-two pound second place fish. He said, "This fish is delicious. I never knew fish could be so good. It must be because it is so fresh, out of the water and into the frying pan."

We all worked up an appetite and devoured that entire fish. There were some hushpuppies left over and a little coleslaw. The fish was so good we just couldn't stop and eating outside made it taste even better.

Dr. Hughes was having the time of his life talking to all these teenagers. He loves giving advice, that's what makes him such a good doctor. He began like this, "Children most often take the same path as their parents. You young ones must keep that in mind as you razzle dazzle each other and become parents. I believe it is always best to set goals on how to do things before a situation is at hand. Raising children is a tremendous obligation and if you get off on the right foot you can save yourselves a lot of heartache. Take Zack for example, he is very hard headed as I'm sure all of you know, since you are his friends, me and the wife were very careful not to break his spirit. The Bible says to spare the rod is to spoil the child. When Zack was young we had to put a switch to his backside a couple of times, he learned early that bad behavior resulted with a switching that stings. He has been a pretty good kid every since. Too many parents either don't address bad behavior at all or go overboard with punishment. No child should ever be hit in the face by a parent, it breaks their spirit, and when they become adults they will know that what you did was wrong and they will rebel, which will damage your relationship with them. However you must take into account the resiliency of the human spirit, that with enough therapy you both may get past this thing. If you do it right, you won't have to spend half of your life in therapy with thousands of dollars lost. Being a good parent makes you an automatic success in life. I tell you this now because until you are near fifty years old, you don't know that the only thing in life that is really important is your family, your children. I'm so proud of Zack that if the joy in my heart were a balloon it would burst. This is a teachable moment, and I want to leave one bit of real truth with each of you, in life the devil may suggest it but we have to do it and own it. The old saying the devil made me do it is not so, it should be the devil suggested I do it and I did, I sinned against God. I want each of you to live in a state of grace, a higher level of existence. Your children will benefit from your gracious role model behavior. We want to send our children out into this world to be men and women, not monsters of their raising. Some are able to rise above their raising, but others become a burden to society. Don't let yourselves be guilty of your neglect to your children."

With a twinkle in his eye, Zack said, "Thank you dad." Mrs. Hughes said, "Exquisitely put."

Chapter 4

Stickball

My dad is very traditional when it comes to our Cherokee heritage. Every year he and mom practice the game of stickball, sometime referred to as "little brothers of war," for two weeks before the games begin. This year the games are being held at Sallisaw to promote the Cherokee culture. In the game wooden sticks with a net at the bottom, which holds a ball, are used to compete. One flings this ball at a wooden fish on the top of a pole, on one end of the field. The opposing team also has a wooden fish on a pole, on the opposite end of the field, which we try to hit with our ball.

In the past I always just watched, but this year I'm competing, and I've asked Zack to be my partner. Zack will be using a stick just like dad, but my mom and myself are allowed to use our hand if we want, because we are females. This game makes for a lot of fun, and couples begin to bond with one another. After the couples game of stickball there is a man's only competition, and the women compete with the pots and pans. It's a competitive cook off just in their minds. There's no prizes or even an official competition, you can just tell each woman wants her dish to be better than the others. I will be making fry bread and my mother will make her famous corn with yellow squash. Dad's good friend will bring a hog, that's right a whole hog, because so many of the players help rebuild his barn last year when a tornado destroyed it. It's his way of showing appreciation for the kindness. He cooks this hog, which weights 400 pounds, in the ground with corn shucks on top to keep it moist. We will eat all our tummy's can hold and divide the rest to take home and freeze, for easy to cook future meals.

Mom and dad were already practicing stickball when Zack came through the backyard gate. He gave Bam a scratch behind the ear and said to her, "That fawn is really growing, when is it due." Bam stuck the ground with her foot three times and Zack said, "Bam are you telling me it will be three months and the fawn will be born." "Zack Bam always does that when you stop scratching behind her ear. That's her way of saying, more please," I said.

I explained the rules concerning stickball to Zack and we joined mom and dad in the backyard. Dad said, "Glad you could make it Zack. There is a stick for you over by the bench."

Zack is a natural athlete, and his agility with the stick is amazing all of us. To watch him, you would think he has played this game all his life. My dad was impressed with how Zack was able to scoop the ball up and fling it in one motion, to hit the wooden fish at the top of the pole, like it was nothing at all.

When we arrived at the park where the stickball game would be held, the elders were warming up. Looks to be around 30 people. Dad said, "This will be a great day, fellowship, just being together to share experiences makes strong bonds and comradeship. These are the things that make life good. It's something to look forward to every year with the same people. Good games, good food, and most of all, good stories.

We arrived early and as we practiced stickball, more and more people were arriving. A total of 55 players arrived when the game began. Some were observers only, but most all played at some point in the game. Some of the elders were able to play for only 15 minutes at a time, when they left the field another would take their place. Everyone old enough to play, waved a stick in the air. The young people watched and got a good laugh at watching their parents play. I remember when I sat and watched mom and dad play stickball, now I'm playing.

I got pushed down a couple of times, and I just could not bring myself to be aggressive to my elders. They could sense this and got a kick out of my humble ways. Zack is much stronger so they could not knock him down, but he was very respectful of his elders also. We played the entire time and loved every minute of it. My mom and dad were in heaven. Most of these people have been their friends all their life, but this is the only time they get to see each other, once a year.

The couple's game is over and everyone is resting. It's time for the elders to share what is going on in their life. Chief Grayhawk started with why we have had such a warm year in 2010.

Chief Grayhawk said, "The magnetic field that surrounds earth from the North Pole to the South Pole are in the process of flipping. The magnetic field, a condition in a region of space, as that around a magnet or an electric current, marked by the existence of a detectable magnetic force at every point in the region, keeps space debris from hitting earth. The magnetic dip which is the angle that the earth's magnetic field makes with the horizontal plane at any given location will be completely gone during the time the North Pole and South Pole are switching magnetic fields. The earth will be vulnerable to a solar flair while the switch of the magnetic field occurs, there will be no magnetic field to stop the solar flair. If this were to occur, all transformers will blow and our infrastructure as we know it will be gone. All satellites will be rendered useless. This means all communication with cell phones end. The gas pumps stop working. Credit cards will be useless because machines will be down. We must be prepared if this scenario were to take place. The first thing we must all do is put in pumps to manually bring water out of the ground. We need clean water to survive. We need an underground protection for potato's, onions, and canned goods. They last a long time in root cellars. We must have solar hot water tanks if we want warm baths. It could take month's to get the infrastructure back in place. We must be prepared to survive this solar flare if it comes during the reversal of the earth's magnetic fields. The earth is 4.6 billion years old and it will survive, the question is, will we survive?"

This was certainly something to think about. We have a spring feed pond, but is the water something we want to drink. Water from under the ground is much cleaner. Mother earth is 2/3water, but most of which is seawater, which we cannot drink.

The air seemed different with the knowledge we gained, the mood drew dark as what Chief Grayhawk said began to sink in to all who understood the effects of a prediction by the National Academy of Science. We all understand that a aurora which is an extreme magnetic solar flair at the North Pole occurs as one of the seven wonders of the world, but most of us were unaware that the magnetic field flips, and during that time that it flips the earth has no protection from sun flares.

Aurora borealis are luminous bands or streamers of light that are sometimes visible in the night skies of the northern regions and are held to be caused by the ejection of charged particles into the magnetic field of the earth. That means the particles got through. That means an asteroid, which is any of numerous celestial bodies with typical diameters between one and several hundred miles and orbits lying chiefly between Mars and Jupiter, would hit earth. It's a scary thought.

With all that knowledge of my future, I'm thinking of

things that will help me and mine get through this possible ordeal while I'm preparing my fry bread. If there is no gas because all gas stations run on computers, than we will need means of transportation. My thoughts are going in all directions. Chief Grayhawk has really got my attention. Do we need to get a horse or would three bicycles be better. You don't have to feed a bicycle, could that be what we need. We could get solar lights and cut down some trees for heat in the fireplace, if this happened in the winter. I know we can come up with a plan if we put our heads together. People survived before all the technologies existed, we can do this. I do think it is best however, to have a plan in place.

The guys are playing for blood now that all the women are cooking. It's brutal what they are doing to each other. Zack will never get all those grass stains out of his clothes. Dad is having the time of his life. Dad's friends are very like-minded. Rough and tumble is their motto.

The game of stickball has come to an end and the guys are giving each other pats on the back and saying things like, good game, what a workout, and we got to do this again soon.

The cooking is done and everyone is grabbing a plate and forming lines. The twenty feet of tables packed with food is a feast fitting for "little brothers of war." Everyone has worked up an appetite and the cooks are bursting with pride each time someone dips an utensil into the dish they prepared. The women really put their heart and soul into their cuisine.

Zack followed close behind me as we filled our plates, Zack said, "Look at those spare ribs, the meat is falling off the bones." I'm so glad Zack is having the time of his life. He is a perfect fit for this lifestyle.

Each person gave thanks for their meal and the fellowship this day brings before they take their first bite. It makes you aware of the goodness our creator provides for each of us if we are willing to make it happen. Friends and food feed the soul, and this is a recipe for true happiness for the day.

"You make a mean fry bread Chelsea, and Mrs. Songbird, this fresh corn scraped off the cob is amazingly good. I've never had anything like it," Zack said. "It's the butter and ground peppercorn that set's it off," said mom.

"These ribs are full of meat, I've never had any ribs this good. The meat is falling off the bone. The smoke flavor makes it where I don't even want any sauce, just the natural flavor of the meat is all I need," dad said.

After the super was over and the dishes were put away, young natives appeared out of nowhere dressed in full feather to do a rain dance. This has been one of the hottest driest summers that any of us could remember and all the grasses and leaves on the trees are showing the effects. Hopefully these young warriors will be able to bring in the clouds to give up their moisture, which we so desperately need. Thoughts of the pear tree that came from a seed off of Jeff's tree came to my mind as the dance progressed. I have been watering this tree every three days to be sure it survives this drought. It has the greenest leaves of any tree on our place right now. Jeff would be proud of the way I have taken care of it. It only has a few pears but they will be good come September. These pears will feed my muscles.

After the dance was over, everyone said there good-by's and we were off to the house. When we got their Zack said, "Look guys I really need a shower so I think I'll be on my way." "I've got some shorts and a tee shirt you can use if you want to use the outdoor shower under the stars. If you get pulled over looking like you do you might get taken in for questioning, besides we would like you to stick around for a couple of hours," dad said.

With that Zack was in the shower and wearing dad's clothes. Since he is company he goes first. Mom and I took inside showers and dad used the outside shower after Zack was finished. In 30 minutes we were all clean as a whistle, sitting in the living room.

"You know Chief Grayhawk had a lot to say tonight about 2013 or a few more years than that. It could be 2025 for all we really know. We should take heed to his words and start preparing. I've been meaning to put that pump in the ground that has been in the barn for two years. Tomorrow I will rent a machine to dig a deep hole by the garden and put that pump in. I got it to save energy by watering the garden but it may be what saves out lives. No human can go very long without water. If a solar flare occurs during the flipping of our magnetic field, everything will be fried that is above ground. That means all the fish on the top part of the lakes and rivers will die in the water and contaminate it for weeks, could even be months. I've always wanted a root cellar and this year will be a good time to put one in. I will do some water witching tomorrow to find the wettest spot to avoid and have it dug next week. I think it will be rather large, I want us to be able to store some wheat in large barrels. Wheat hold's it's nutritional value for seven years if stored properly. All you need to do is add water and you can survive for a long time on wheat. The fish that go deep in the lakes will survive and they also will be a source of food in time. I will put rods and reels with plenty of string in the root cellar. We can take a pair of Quail to raise their offspring's for the future, they won't need a lot of wheat seeds and they will fit in the root cellar. I've been meaning to put in a solar hot water tank to save on energy, looks like another project that needs to be put in high gear," dad said.

"I think three bicycles with spare tires and a pump and patches would be a smart thing for transportation. All the tires will be melted off of the cars, and a bicycle will fit in the root cellar," I said.

"I want to thank this family for taking me to this event of Stickball, great food, fellowship, and for saving my life. Because of you I was able to hear Grayhawk, I mean Chief Grayhawk, tell me about the possible end of life as we know it. I will be doing everything you have talked about today with my family. Mr. Songbird, I would like to help you put in your manual water pump tomorrow," Zack said. Dad just nodded his head in agreement and put up eight fingers, for the time.

Eight o'clock came early in the morning, probably because we had such an eventful day yesterday. Mom had breakfast already cooked and Zack was knocking on the door. After we all had breakfast, dad and Zack were off to the rental store for the equipment to dig a hole, with coffee cups in hand. No time to waste today.

In two hours time the pump was in the ground and working. Dad put the pump at the edge of the garden so we could use it for watering the garden instead of running water from our well, which requires electricity. Dad plans to place an attachment that will run water through the soaker hoses to distribute the water evenly in the garden.

Zack called his dad, Dr. Hughes to see if he had picked up his pump, so it could be installed today while the machine to dig the hole was available. Zack said, "Dad has a pump and he is ready to install it. When I told him about what Chief Grayhawk had to say he let me know that it's better to be prepared, that way you don't live in fear. You have a plan, if the worst were to happen."

Dad was home four hours later, and he was impressed with Zack's family. Dad made comments about how they are a lot like us. How they value the family, they educate their children on politics and the importance of having a relationship with God.

"The world is a better place because of people like these," Dad said. Dr. Hughes believes if you fail your family you are a failure in life, I could not agree with him more. "By the way, after the solar flare is over, Dr. Hughes said that we can borrow Zack to noodle some catfish for the super table," Dad said.

Chapter 5
Back to School

Tomorrow is the first day of school and I'm super excited about seeing my friends, that is, my friends who are at a distance. People that say hello, as we pass in the halls of the school, on our way to the next class, but we don't hang out. People that I haven't seen all summer.

Senior year has a final feeling to it, of it all being over except for the reunions every five years or so. I know this will be my best year ever with the Prom, and having a car and the freedom it brings to go to football games, and all my friends calling for a ride to party's and other events. It's just exciting to be so grown up and having 300 seniors all going their own way after this last year of high school.

BreAnna called and we talked in detail about what we would be wearing the first day of school. "I have a pink top that is stretch with a white collar that stands up in the back. This pink top is long so one time I can wear it tucked in side my jeans and the next time I can wear it out where it covers almost to my knees. It is so thin it's like a body suit. I bought a pair of white stretch jeans at the mall today that will work perfect with this top. They are called skinny jeans. Seldom do I find jeans that are to long for me, but these I will have to roll up. I got a new pair of white patent leather shoes with just a slight heel on them. I don't want to look taller than most of the guys. I'm going to pull my hair up on top of my head and put a white hair clamp in to hold it in place. I have a arm bag purse that fits on my arm with Velcro that holds my cell phone, drivers license, money, and keys. It is so convenient and it gives me comfort to look at my arm and know everything I need is right their. It is also stretch and light as a feather. If you don't put a lot of things in it you don't even know it is there," BreAnna said.

BreAnna's excitement is rubbing off on me. I'm wearing clothes from last year but I'm wearing my hair up on top of my head after talking to BreAnna. That should give me a grown up look. Heads will be turning saying 'who is that?'

My internal clock got me out of bed before the alarm went off. I love it when that happens. I just seem more rested when I wake up on my own. I have a little stretching routine I go through every morning before my day starts and today I'm reaching for the sky in the backyard. It is a beautiful day to start school. The birds are singing and the air is moist, with a light fog. The rays of the sun are peaking through the leaves that have turned yellow from the hot summer we are having. The morning glory flowers somehow have managed to keep brilliant blue color despite the heat. As I gaze upon the wonders of nature Bam is emerging from the wildlife refuge. She is approaching in a slow gallop to greet me. As she approaches I reminisce about the first time I set eyes on her. She was in the arms of my dad's friend and my mom brought out a bamboo basket with a white towel in it for her bed. I took her from the arms of dad's friend and placed her in her new bed. It was like 'Bam' what a beautiful sight. That's how she got her name. I thought about calling her bamboo after her bed, but Bam fit best. Maybe I will call her fawn Bamboo, or just Boo. As Bam nears she slows down and her ears and tail begin to twitch. She is as excited as me, this morning. I think we well both have a wonderful day.

It's time for my first day of school, as I park my Mustang I notice Zack getting out of his truck. He spots me about the same time and I wave him over. We walk through the doors together. As we go our separate ways to first hour, I said, "See you at lunch."

Everyone looks so grown up, not just bigger but the way they carry themselves. Everyone seems to have more confidence. I wonder if they are thinking the same way about me, with my hair up on top of my head and all. I wonder if they had as much fun this summer as I did. Do they have part time jobs, are they driving cars?.

Last year was a daze, with Jeff's accident and all the sadness I experienced, but this year will be different. I know Jeff will continue to improve and I have the courage to let him go. I think if I started dating it would help me move on.

First hour is Algebra II and it will not be easy. The book is large and the problems look to be challenging. This year the school has provided a tutor for students who have difficultly with math. We can make an appointment one hour before class or two hours after class.

On my way to my second hour class a student named Carl came up behind me and started some small talk, he must have grown three inches over the summer.

"I seen you driving into the parking lot this morning in that hot Mustang, I was in a truck beside you. I started to honk but thought it might startle you. Have you been driving long?" Carl said.

I said, "A little over a year, but I've put a lot of miles on the road, they add up to a lot of experience. Thanks for not honking your horn, it would have startled me."

"Chelsea, I would like for you to watch me practice for track after school. It will only last for 30 minutes. You would be an inspiration for me to run faster. Will you come? Afterwards we could go for a coke or just ride around for a while," Carl said.

"Sounds like fun, I'll be there," I said. I'm having a blast seeing all the teens that have matured over the summer.

Everyone seems to be more flirty than last year. Must be all the hormones I've been hearing so much about. There is a lot going on in my life and knowing that Jeff has learned to tie his shoe string has given me strength and the inspiration to live life to it's full measure. We never know what is lerking around the corner for us.

We all must learn to be more flexible and resilient. This will lead to being more self-aware so we can re-examine our priorities. We should repeat the good we learn from life like Jeff is doing. It's hard for me to wrap my mind around the idea that Jeff is so excited that he has learned to tie his shoe-string and he is self-aware of something we don't even think about when we do it. That's the difference of being self-aware and going through the act mindlessly.

All these hormones going around school this year has me thinking about the effect that Jeff had on me at one time. He is a different person now and I respect his request that I leave him alone. Jeff is being home schooled and I look forward to the day he catches up with others his age. I know his parents are doing everything in their power to help Jeff's recovery.

This year BreAnna and Jake have joined us for lunch, in the cafeteria. I was the first to sit down, than Angela and Sara and right behind them, Brad and Zack. BreAnna and Jake were the last to arrive, and they sat side by side, at times they were leaning into each other's shoulders.

Everyone is eating extremely healthy today. We all have a salad and baked chicken. The veggies vary, we all have adopted Jeff's idea of becoming centenarians, and diet plays a major role to achieve this goal.

Angela said, "The food is better this year or maybe I'm just making better choices. Hey Chelsea, by the way, I saw you talking to Carl this morning. He must have grown three inches since I seen him last."

I said, "Yes he has grown a lot. He is on the track team

this year and has asked me to watch him practice today. I'm going to check it out and observe Carl's skills."

"You better watch yourself with Carl, he doesn't take judgment very well, especially if you find fault in him. He is a hot head and it doesn't take much to set him off. However, I think he will be good at running in track for he can take all his frustrations out on the track. I think it will help him release some of his anger. You just be careful with him Chelsea," Brad said.

My friends are just looking out for my welfare. That's so sweet. Guys know each other way better than girls do in the beginning. As time goes on things change because girls get to see the vulnerable side of guys that they would never let their buddies see. It's a guy thing.

Zack said, "Chelsea, I'm having baseball practice just the other side of where the track team runs, if you want you can get a glance at my ability to knock one out of the park."

I nodded in acceptance of Zack's invitation. Lunch was ending and we all took off in the direction of our Advanced Government class. This is so neat that we get to spend an hour and a half together and get a great education at the same time.

The first day of school has been a blast, and now it's time to watch Carl run on the track team. When I arrived Carl was stretching to prevent any muscles from cramping up. He noticed me and waved in acknowledgement of my presence. I waved back. On the other side of the bleachers the baseball team was warming up. I climbed to the top of the bleachers so I could watch Zack bat the ball and Carl run for his life at the same time. My head was turning back and forth like I was afraid I might miss a big moment in the life of these two guys.

After practice Carl waved me down from the bleachers and said, "Let's go get something to drink." He just kept walking and I had to rush around to catch up. Carl unlocked the door to the truck but failed to open the door. It almost felt rude. I thought, maybe I'm overreacting; he is just tired from running and not thinking clear. When I got into the truck Carl said, "Did you enjoy watching the baseball team? For some reason I thought you were there to watch me run."

I said, "I did come to watch you run, a good friend of mine, Zack, is on the baseball team and he also invited me to watch him play. We have been good friends for a long time." Carl got very quite and I began to feel uncomfortable. It is as if he is upset that I watched Zack part of the time. Carl pulled into a drive-in, rolled down the window and ordered two cokes. He did not even ask me what I wanted to drink. I was to the point that I just wanted this to be over with. I took the coke in order to not upset Carl. I would have preferred a cup of water, I don't even drink coke. The silence was like thunder cracking open the sky. I have to take control of this situation so I said, "You look to be the fastest on the team, are you?" Carl said, "You noticed." I replied, "Yes, you left everyone behind. You will earn some metals for your letter jacket if you keep up your stride like you ran today."

Carl liked being bragged on and he was beaming with a smile that filled his face. His whole attitude changed and the negative vibe left the air as quickly as it had filled the air. I guess he just wanted all my attention. This is something he will have to change if he wants to be around me. I'm a very social person and friends mean a lot to me. He will just have to adjust if we spend much time together.

The rest of the day was very pleasant. Carl has a good personality and I enjoyed the time we spent together. The next day as I pulled into the schools parking lot, Carl was right behind me in his truck. When he got out of his truck he said, "Hey Chelsea we better hurry or we will be late for class." We walked side by side into the building and I could feel many eyes upon us. Are all these students thinking that Carl and myself are a couple? Is this his intention? Carl is a very handsome guy and built very lean which is perfect for a runner. I know he will be successful in his endeavors in track. Sports contribute to popularity simply because it gets one's name out their when they excel at whatever sport they are a part of. This is very important to Carl because he is self-absorbed in his image. I don't want to be used for anyone's image, so my eyes are wide open right now.

Carl insisted that I walk with him to his class, since it was only a few steps out of the way to my first hour class. The whole time his eyes were darting back and forth to see how many students were taking notice of whom he was with. I almost winded up being late for class. I was the last student to set down at my desk. The girl setting behind me said, "Are you and Carl an item." I just shook my head to indicate, no. As the day went on a couple of more students hit me with the same question. It is amazing how fast things like this get around. I'm not going to over react to this situation, for it would only bring more attention to it. I will simply reply with a simple shake of my head to indicate a no. By the time lunch had started all of my friends have been made aware that I walked Carl to his first hour class.

Angela said, "I understand you walked Carl to his first hour class today. Stories have it that he has swept you off your feet." I raised my eye brow a couple of times and said, "Carl is quite handsome and would be considered a good catch for someone who is shallow enough to think it is the most important trait to date someone for, however, I'm still just getting to know him and haven't decided if we are a good match yet. We are going to dinner Saturday and this should help me to get to know him better." All my friends at the lunch table snickered a little and then changed the subject.

Carl continued to show up in the school parking lot so I could walk him to his first hour class. When he would call me on the phone, he seemed to talk only about himself. This is definitely helping me to get to know him. I wonder when he will run out of things to say about himself.

Saturday night has the sweet smell of rain in the air. Carl was on time, but instead of coming to the door, he honked his horn for me to go to his truck. I was so taken by the honking of his horn that I forgot my umbrella. As we were driving to the restaurant the rain began to fall. The parking lot was full of cars so we had to park far from the entrance of the restaurant. Carl opened his umbrella and said that we could share. When he got out of the truck he just headed for the door to the restaurant and must have expected me to catch-up, which was difficult seeing how I'm not on the track team like Carl. By the time I made it to the door, I was drenched. Carl said, "Theirs the guys, come on were late for the game. It has already started."

Carl handed me a couple of napkins to dry off with and started talking to his friends about the football game on the oversized screen hanging on the wall. It was as if I didn't exist. Everyone, including Carl, was glued to the game. When the waiter took our order, Carl didn't even ask what I wanted to eat, he just ordered for me. This was insulting but I refused to let myself make a seen. I kept my cool and just nibbled at the fried food he ordered for me.

When the evening came to an end and Carl was driving me home, I was quiet, not a word came out of my mouth. This was great for Carl, he talked about himself the entire drive to my house. When we pulled into the driveway it was my turn to talk. I said, "Carl, I don't think we have much in common, and before I could finish what I was saying, Carl's lips were upon mine and his strong arms would not let me pull away. When he released me, I just opened the door to his truck and let myself out. Carl called out to me as I walked to my house, "See you Monday morning."

I was spitting Carl out of my mouth as he pulled out of the driveway. I want nothing more to do with this self-absorbed person. Who does he think he is? Forcing himself upon me. He best stay away from me.

I had no idea that such a person even existed on earth.

Carl seems to only be aware of himself and his wants. How boorish and rude a person is he? I want nothing more to do with him. What Carl needs is a shallow person who is only concerned with how handsome he is, not how self-absorbed his personality is for his needs only.

The next morning Angela called to see if I wanted to go to church with her. Somehow she knew what an awful time I had on that date with Carl. Angela did not mention the date until after church was over. Then Angela said to me, "How was your date with Carl." "Simple awful," I replied. Angela said, "After what Brad said to you at lunch last week, I thought you may not have much fun. My understanding is that Carl is into himself. In Matthew 10-39, "He who seeks only himself brings himself to ruin, whereas he who brings himself to naught for me discovers who he is." Another passage in Mathew 7-6 "Do not give what is holy to dogs or toss your pearls before swine. They will trample them under foot, at best, and perhaps even tear you to shreds." These are powerful messages from God Himself. Until Carl see's the light you best avoid his advances."

Angela somehow knew what I was going through with Carl. She had these passages ready to quote for me. She did not call Carl a swine, but pigs are known to be very selfish. Carl is all about his ego, and that is ugly to me. In just one week Carl has managed to steal my dignity. I keep telling myself things would get better once Carl got to know me better but instead it just got worse. When he couldn't even share his umbrella, and let me get soaked by the rain, I realized things would reach an all time low in my life if I allowed it to. If Carl had any sensitivity at all, he'd know how I was feeling, unhappy with great humiliation. In the beginning I was intrigued by his presence and overwhelmed by his good looks and smooth approach, but that is all gone now that I got to know him.

Everything is wrong about the two of us and I intend to

address this Monday morning when he pulls up in his truck. I don't know how I could have let it get this far out in the beginning. It's not like me to let anyone treat me the way Carl did. It's best if I just admire him from a distance, both physically and emotionally. I am attracted to how Carl looks but never could I allow him to continue to treat me like he has.

Angela was emphatic with all the ill treatment I've experienced this week and she is letting me vent all my frustration. She is a great listener.

Monday morning as I pulled into the schools parking lot Carl was nowhere around. I was ready to let him know I had no more interest in being around him. I felt disappointed for I had my lines all ready for him and in the parking lot where no one would see what was going on. I waited until time was running out and if I waited any longer I would be late for class. I locked my car and looked around the parking lot for Carl, he was nowhere in sight. I walked in the door of the school, and Carl walked up behind me and said, "Good morning beautiful." He startled me and I was surprised by his voice. No way was he going to get me to make a scene in front of all these students. I began to bite my tongue to keep my words in my mouth. Instead of walking to his class I passed right by it and went to my class. Carl was right beside me saying slow down a little. I kept my pace and walked into my classroom without a word coming out of my mouth. I refuse to let Carl upset me ever again.

The day was moving slow and I was ready for lunch, my friends always make things better on the worst of days. When I sat down at the lunch table no one mentioned Carl. There was a lot of talk about what everyone had done over the weekend, but no one asked how my weekend went and I was grateful for that. Zack walked me to our Advanced Government class and I appreciated his presence.

The next day Carl was nowhere in sight. My silence spoke volumes and obviously Carl got the message.

Chapter 6
Advanced Government

This class has opened my eyes to the importance of having knowledge of the officials that we elect to our Senate and Congress. They have the power to add amendments, which are a revision of what they believe to be an improvement, to our founder's constitution. The United States constitution is a system of fundamental laws and principles that prescribes the nature, function, and limits of an institution, as a government. We must not let the government add amendments to the point we don't even recognize what the word freedom means. If the people of the United States don't recognize the fact that they are being robbed of their freedoms by the very men and women who they elected for office, the United States of America will become a third world country. The only way to keep this from happening is to elect people for office on their values, not on how much money they have spent on their campaign. We must know how they vote on issues that could cost us our freedom, and way of life.

To keep our freedom, government must have limits. We have plenty of law's, we don't need new ones just so someone can look like they are doing their job. Beware of elected officials looking to make a name for their self at your expense.

George Washington, our first president, followed rules for civil behavior from the time he was a young gentleman, all the way through his presidency. These rules provided the discipline that lead to his positions of leadership through out his life. These rules consisted of the importance of honesty, respect, courtesy and humility. With these rules close to his heart he achieved honor, something money will never buy. Because of the rules of civil behavior that he put in place for himself, people gave him the respect that a president must have in order to be an effective commander-in-chief of the armed forces.

Our teacher shows a fondness for our first President, George Washington, who was offered to be a King by the people. He wanted more for the people, he wanted them to rule the government, not the government rule the people. This is what sets us as a nation apart from the rest of the world. This is what makes America special, we the people rule ourselves by who we put in office.

Zack believes laws should be made to protect people from harm, not to protect wild animals, or fish, or chickens that we eat. Dogs and cats, are not wild animals, they are domesticated and fall into a completely different category. People who donate money for domesticated animals should demand their money is spent on preventing reproduction of unwanted dogs and cats, not on wages for someone looking to make a criminal out of a person who is hunting for the food to feed their children, or someone who raises food for the grocery store and has to kill the animal and clean it for us to eat. It is Zack's opinion that all money donated to the welfare of dogs and cats should go directly to the vets so they may prevent unwanted new born domesticated animals from being harmed. This would solve 90% of the problems with unwanted pets by people who cannot afford to pay for the surgery necessary to prevent unwanted pets.

Our teacher encourages the class to express ourselves on subjects that would improve the process of our government. Laws are very difficult to change once they get on the books so we must all stay active in the process of law making. We must not let things go, thinking that someone else will take care of it because we think it is wrong. We must take an active interest in thing that are of importance to us because a law can change our way of life over night.

The subject of import tax became the focal point for today's class. Jake has taken a stand on the problem of lack of high paying jobs in the United States. Jake believes that 60% of products should be made in the United States and 40% could be made over seas. If they build 100% overseas than a large import tax should be applied to the product. This would drive down the deficit and breath new life into our economy.

Jake talked about how all the college students graduating from college and getting a degree are unable to get a decent job. The American dream is fading and something must be done before the light goes out. We are not talking about getting a job we are talking about getting a decent paying job.

Jake is committed to become active in politics on his 18th birthday, and challenged the class to do the same. He plans to begin with volunteering at the State Capital for hands on experience. Jake first wants to become a state legislature and become involved in the lawmaking of Oklahoma. After he gets his feet wet he plans to run for Congress and than the Senate. Jake wants to make our country the best place in the world to live, now and in the future.

The next day Brad was up on his soapbox. Brad said, "I plan to become a DEA agent and protect our children from drug pushers. Protecting our children from becoming drug addicts, or dying from overdoses should be the number one thing on every lawmakers mind. They are the future generation that will be protecting this great country. Drugs take away young peoples values. We don't need a generation of people who have no values, running this great nation.

It is my opinion we need to improve this process of controlling what is happening to our children, because of drug pushers. This is where we need more laws, to protect human beings from the monsters who want to steal their souls.

I believe the answer to solving the problem is through increasing our intelligence forces. With all the tools we have because of the internet and cell phones, we should be making more of an impact in the war on drugs. If we need tougher laws for the drugs that cause addiction, than so be it."

Sounds to me like Brad will make a great lawmaker. I believe tough laws to protect all people from the poison of addictive drugs is a must if we want to remain a free nation. Drugs will be the ruination of our youth if we chose to ignore the rise of addictive drugs on our streets.

The teacher took back control of the class and returned to his favorite subject George Washington, and his contribution to our great nation. Washington believed that the people should control their government not the government rule the people. The only way for this to happen is to keep government small. If you have for example, 80% of the people working in government jobs, these people will vote to secure their jobs and the government will own the country. Freedom will have been bought for the price of a job. Encouraging small business is the only way to keep this from happening. Competition automatically controls pricing and the cost of goods become affordable through competition between businesses. Lower taxes means more money for the consumer to buy goods with.

George Washington laid the foundation for freedom and we must never let it be stolen from us. We have the greatest country on earth, because, it is run by, 'We the people.' This must never be forgot.

George Washington loved the great outdoors and spent

time fox hunting and fishing. He believed every man owned the right to the pursuit of happiness as long as it is not at the expense of mankind's safety. Our teacher challenged us to learn everything we can about George Washington so we can understand what he wanted for this great country of ours, 'freedom.' He left us with the words, "Just because someone wants to make a law that takes away a persons freedom, and pursuit of happiness, we don't have to let it happen. We must protect every person's freedom even if we don't like noodling for a catfish. We must protect those who do like noodling, with our power of the vote."

The class got a good laugh out of the teacher standing up for Zack and his beloved sport.

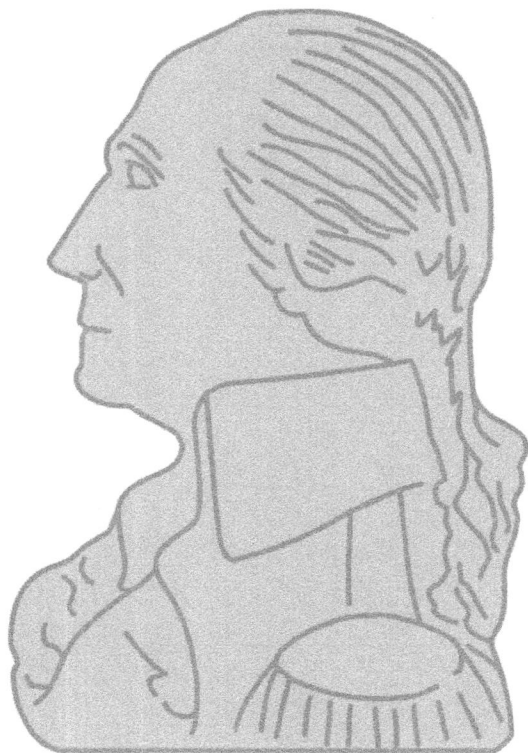

Chapter 7
Biology

The teacher began the lecture with, "Human beings are multicellular, or in other words made from numerous cells. You see, cells are the basic units of life, and all cells come from preexisting cells. The structure and form of the body comes from these cells. This is why children will have features from both their father and mother. Sometimes they even have the personality of one of the parents.

Multicellular humans begin life as a single cell; they grow to a certain size and then divide, forming tissues. In this tissue is hereditary information that is carried from one generation to the next. That is why DNA evidence at a crime scene will have characteristic of almost the whole family of either the victim or the person whom committed the crime. With this information the police are able to solve many more crimes than ever in the history of mankind.

Because our DNA defines who we are, we can see ourselves in our grandparents and great, great grandparents. Our DNA can be improved through the nourishment of our cells, with proper nutrition, and our intelligence through education. With the proper raising of children, through nurture, which is your upbringing and rearing, each generation of the family will improve. Much like a seed of corn put into the ground that is cultivated by removing weeds, and fertilized, and watered, will produce plump kernel of corn for planting the following season. These same seeds can be planted in poor soil with weeds choking them out, and they will produce small kernels of corn, which are more likely to succumb to a disease.

If human beings nourish their child's cells with the enzymes found in vegetables and meats the future generations could possible live a healthier life. An enzyme is any of numerous proteins and functioning as biochemical catalysts in living organisms. By protecting your cells from toxic waste like sugar and white flour, you are protecting your blood and cells which will live in your off springs.

Another way to improve your family trees future is by the mate you choose to marry and have your children with. The infusing of genetically strong healthy DNA will also add to the health of your future family."

My eyes drifted in the direction of where Zack was sitting. We are just really good friends, but he definitely has good DNA. His family is well educated and they believe in a balanced diet. He would be a perfect match for me, and my future family if we became a married couple. He looks at me as just a friend but I can see us as more than just friends, I guess when I kissed him it felt right for me. Zack didn't make a big deal out of it so it must be a one sided feeling.

Zack must have felt me looking at him because his eyes locked onto mine before I could turn my head. As my head began to turn, my eyes stayed on Zack until they were on the side of my head. Zack just gave me a sly smile and turned his head back to the front of the room where the teacher is lecturing.

The teacher had moved on to the importance of vaccine for disease such as smallpox. "When the European colonized North America the Indian population declined because of the initial contact with the Spanish. Europeans suffered major epidemics in the preceding centuries and were immune to the diseases they carried. Native Americans had never been exposed to smallpox and many died during the epidemic. We now vaccinate to keep infection and outbreaks of epidemics for future generations, under control. No matter how healthy you are, if you come in contact with certain viruses, you can become infected. Vaccination is the way to protect yourself and your family. Some people think vaccines cause autism, but others think chemicals such as arsenic cause autism. It is a problem that needs answers for sure.

The first vaccine was prepared from the virus that causes cowpox, as the derivation of the word vaccine from Latin vacca, "cow," might suggest. Cowpox is a mild disease of cows that can be caught by human beings. In the late 18th century, Dr. Edward Jenner discovered that someone who has had cowpox is almost always immune to smallpox, a related, but much more serious disease. Jenner invented a method of inoculating human beings with the cowpox virus and he called the inoculating agent "vaccine." Since that time many other diseases have been prevented by inoculation, and the word vaccine has been applied to the inoculating agent in all such cases.

That's all for today class. Next week we will dissect a frog so you can see the inside organs and muscles of what was a live reptile," the teacher said.

As the class filed out the door, Zack was behind me and said, "Chelsea, I really like this class, how about you." I said, "Yes it is very interesting and probably the most important class as far as protecting ourselves and our future family. In the old days a lot of parents chose their children's mates. They had all the knowledge about genes, what we call DNA now, and wanted the best for their children. However there is one thing left out of the mix, and that is love, the most important thing in a marriage. With Biology, young people will have the knowledge to choose what is best for them."

We all made good choices in the lunch line to feed our cells. This Biology class is just re-enforcing what all of us knew about the importance of a balanced diet. I was the first in line and selected a spinach and cabbage salad with a boiled egg sliced in half. For desert a container of strawberries and yogurt, and a half of cantaloupe. As I looked behind me, every one of my friends are selecting the exact same choices that I made. When we sat down we all looked at each other and began giggling. Angela said, "My cells should be happy today. If I wind up marring Brad my children will be strong, but will probably spend a lot of time in summer school playing catch up." The whole table laughed out loud. Brad just turned bright red and Angela gave him a hug. It was said in fun, not malice.

As we all finished our healthy meal, BreAnna said, "I hope the world is ready for Jake and BreAnna's offspring, we are talking about a very intelligent and athletic kid or should I say kids." Sara said, "Is there something you two are trying to tell us." Jake and BreAnna both put up their hands that are wearing their celibacy rings, which means they practice abstinence. Jake said, "Yea, were telling you we will be getting married when we turn 24 years old. We plan to have four children and hope they have half my traits and half of her traits. They will have the best of both worlds. Not to brag, but we both have a lot to offer, thanks to God's blessing." Sara jumped into the conversation and said, "I have yet to pick a lifetime mate, but I have a charming personality to contribute to my off-springs and the ability to nurture my off-springs so they will have the confidence to make a productive and happy life for themselves."

Zack just looked at me, and me at him, with a glimpse into our possible future in total silence. Zack is a perfect mate for me but we are just friends. Zack doesn't look at me as a girl friend; he looks at me as a friend only. I keep saying that. However, we would have the perfect family, with his muscles and my agile ability, which is able to move quickly, nimble, and being mentally alert. I have a lot to offer. We both have strong family values, which is the most important thing to a family. Values are what make your kids good kids. If your children get into trouble because they lack values, everyone suffers. If my children get in trouble, I don't want it to be because I dropped the ball. I will do everything in my power to nurture my children and give them values that will give them a head start, like my parents gave me. This will ensure happiness for the entire family. If a family member has problems, the whole family feels their pain.

Angela said, "I have a new song that I would like to share with all of you, that is if you would like to hear it, raise your hand if you do. Okay here goes,

Family Treasures

What we think creates our future, molds our children, and forms our soul, bringing us family pleasures.

So free your soul and do what your told, the Bible has the answers to make the family whole.

If your searching for answers, open up the Book, it explores the meaning, you'll find the answers to life lived well.

Your heart is at your own disposal, be swift to secure your happiness, your mind is like the buds that open in the spring morning, pure and sweet to the smell.

The choice fruits of your mind are ripe with thoughts of aroused love; your soul is that of an artist painting a picture of joy and happiness.

How beautiful you are, how pleasing the sound of your voice, how fragrant your breath of truth, which brings true family treasures.

Let us be the seal on your heart for devotion with flaming joy of the love of life that only family can bring.

Deep waters cannot quench love, nor floods sweep it away. We may offer all we own to purchase love, but only a open heart can capture true family love.

We are faint with love and radiant with warmth, for our souls are clean, we will be bringing children in the world to be singing God's name.

For God is the one who brings family pleasures and makes the mind clean.

We live in our minds, we create our own thinking, we are the masters of our minds.

We are a garden fountain, a well of water flowing fresh from our minds, the perfumes of our mind spread love with the smell so sweet, the moisture of the night sends our hearts trembling for the answers to life's family puzzles.

Our hearts blossomed with the sight of good deeds, for this is food for a healthy soul.

We are the watchman of our souls, we drink freely of love of the world, and open our hearts.

What we think creates our future, molds our children, forms our soul, bringing us family pleasures.

So stop your mistakes.

Make time for your family and make the right choices.

Being with my family makes my mind sing, I can't wait until I grow up and my boyfriend gives me a ring, this will be the beginning of my new thing, called family treasures.

This will be the man I will live and die with in my heart, this is where my own family treasures will be born."

"That is a great message Angela, would you like to hear what I've been working on. You know you are not the only talent here," Brad said. "If you think you can top that, knock yourself out," Angela said. Brad responded with "Well here goes,

Yo Teacher

Yo teacher, if you wanta teach me you gotta reach me.

So come on down to my level like fat to lean, we gotta meet in between.

With pounding minds that echo neither warm nor cold we need mind bending knowledge that excites the soul.

Yo teacher, if you wanta teach me you gotta reach me.

Rushing brains will remain stained with thoughts the teacher brought. So teacher beware the mind you faulter will alter your world. Our roaring minds seek sounds of knowledge mirroring the teachers college.

Yo teacher, if you wanta teach me you gotta reach me."

Everyone stood up and cheered for Brad. None of us thought he had it in him, however, Summer school must have agreed with him, he could very well be the next great writer.

Chapter 8

Fly Fishing

Kyle invited the gang to go fly-fishing with him at the mouth of the Illinois River. This river feeds Lake Tenkiller on one end and is released at the other end of the lake below the dam. This is where water comes out from the bottom of the lake and is what Kyle referees to as the mouth of the river. Because the water is released from the bottom of the lake, it is ice cold. Trout love cold water and that is what we are fishing for today.

It is nice to have a fly-fishing pole but not mandatory if the fishing pole is rigged properly for catching trout. Most of the gang have regular fishing poles, however my grand father gave me his bamboo fly rod. I tend to use it more than the graphite rod I brought for myself. I will let Zack use my graphite rod.

The 9-foot bamboo rod my grandfather gave me has a fast recovery rate and that is what I like about it. Also the design of the grip, the cigar handle is perfect for my size hand, and is comfortable when I cast. The drag is perfect, slow and never overruns the spool. This is important when you have a large trout on your line. The reel has an exposed spool rim that I'm able to apply extra drag tension to by pressing my open hand against the rim, in other words I'm palming. The single-action reel is very durable. The line is 110 feet long and floats on top of the water. The line is a size 8, which is light enough to cast at great distance and yet strong enough to catch a large fish. Also the line is light in color so I can detect a strike.

When everyone arrived, Kyle took inventory of the bait, both dry flies and dough bait. Kyle came to the conclusion that the gang needed to talk to his friend Mr. Hawk. He lives with his son but has a building for his business deep in the side of the bluff overlooking the river. The windows give it light that illuminates the hundreds of flies he has made. Every color between black and white, pink and red, and yellow and green lines the walls. Mr. Hawk sells his dry flies to a large distributor twice a year, so he has the largest selection I have ever seen in one place. Mr. Hawk let us know that trout were hitting on the fly with a white body and black wings. Kyle purchased 20 flies from him and distributed them to all of us. As I walked to the window the view of the river below was breathtaking. The sun reflecting on the running water was the color of a rainbow. The water is so clear I can see the fish swimming in packs, and I wonder are they all brother's and sisters. In a pocket on the left bank of the river is a group of very large trout. That's where my line will land. I asked Mr. Hawk if I could use the trail leading down to the river from his cabin. He pointed to the tail and said, "This trail is the one that I take and is the easiest to walk down." I grabbed my pole and headed down the trail, Zack was right behind me. The foliage is as thick as fog and we can only see where the trail has the vegetation cut back. The trail is rocky like stair steps. I look back at the cabin to judge how much further we have to go. The old man is watching me from his window and gives me a wave. Kyle told me about the old man when he invited me to go trout fishing. He said the old man is very wise.

Kyle first met him on the banks of the river early one morning. He was sitting on a bucket with his fly pole in hand and fishing very close to the bank. The old man pulled out three trout that were between 10 and 14 inches long. Kyle, being the curious guy that he is, asked the old man what his secret was for catching trout. The old man responded, "If I told you it would not be a secret any more now would it." Kyle responded, "Let me put it another way, would you be so kind as to give me some pointers, so I can catch one fish today." The old man nodded his head and handed Kyle a bright pink fly and said, "This is what they fancy today." Kyle tied it on and soon caught his limit. The old man pointed to a spot high on the bluff and said, "Do you see that glimmer up there. That's a reflection from a glass window where I make these flies for fishing. Come up sometime and I will give you one of each color. You can try each one until you figure out what color they like for the day. Also, while you are up there, you can see where the larger fish are hanging out. Get a marker like a tree or large rock so when you are down here you know where to throw your line." Kyle said, "Thanks for the info and invite. I will take you up on it."

I took all the information in that Kyle shared with me and looked back at the old gray-headed man with a braid that reached the middle of his back. I wondered how long it took him to grow his hair that long or had it always been long and he just trimmed it occasionally. He was still following us with his eyes as if in anticipation of the big catch we are about to make. By giving us flies that the trout like today, he has a hand in our outcome.

As we made it to the bottom of the bluff I said, "This way Zack, that is the tree where the large trout are swimming. Cast your line just the other side of the boulder." As a fly angler I put on my wading outfit before entering the ice-cold stream. The knots I now tie when making leaders, and connecting them to the fly line comes natural to me. Mom and dad take me fly fishing with them at least six times a year. This is why I have a wading outfit and Zack is fishing from the shoreline. I have studied the behavior of the trout and this gives me an advantage over most fly anglers.

My rod is perfectly controlling my line to land exactly where I intended it to go. What looked like a twelve-inch trout was nibbling at my fly. Knowing when to set the hook is the secret to catching trout. Also the fly must look natural in the water and must float in the same direction as a live fly would float, otherwise the trout will refuse to take the fly. Mr. Hawk's fly is setting perfect on the water. This trout is very interested in the black and white nymph on the end of my line. As my eyes followed the trout, suddenly he took the fly and I set the hook. He was bending my bamboo pole over as he used the current of the river to help him in his escape. No such luck for him today. As I gently back up towards the shore of the river, the trout loses the swift current; he was beginning to lose power. I took him into the shore line to be sure he couldn't flop around and get lose. Zack had a grin on his face as if to say, 'good job'.

The old man definitely let his secret out today about what the trout are eating. The water is very cold today and that makes the trout more active and hungry. It is very early in the morning and that is when the water is the coldest. The sun is not high enough in the sky yet to affect the fish. You see, fish have no eyelids and bright sunlight is harmful to their eyes, especially in clear water. It is in our favor to catch as many trout as possible before noon, when the sun is bright.

Once again I gently cast my fly into the shallow water where I spotted a scowl of rainbow trout swirling around in a frenzied, greedily sucking in tiny insects that were falling into the river. The intensity of a swarm of mayflies above a 20-inch rainbow trout had my heart beating fast. A light rain began bouncing on the river when I seen the dorsal fins right before the savage strike of the rainbow trout. The overcast contributed to his raving hunger. The tiny raindrops woke him form his slumber. He moved my hook. I try once again to land my fly over this monoester of a trout.

Suddenly the large trout violently grabbed the fly insect as it broke the surface of the water with a splash that echoed down the river. The current is swift and the trout is dragging me through hidden depths that are undetected by the eye. The chest waders that I have on give me an advantage by allowing me to get close to the fish and put a net under it before I put myself in danger of wading into an area that I'm unsure of.

I'm eye to eye with this 20-inch trout as I attempt to put the net under him. He fly's out of the water and pulls my pole down. I gain control once again and this time the net is under him and going up into the air with him. He is caught and I head to the bank where Zack is throwing his arms into the air as if he caught the trout himself. A smile was all over my face as I told Zack, "There is nothing more fun than fly fishing, and by the way, that's the biggest rainbow trout I've ever caught." Zack said, "He is the most beautiful fish I've ever seen." "Let me tell you a little bit about trout, they spawn in the winter and in the beginning they live off the yolk sac which gradually disappears. They are much like chickens; they hatch out of an egg. Sara should be crazy about them seeing how she likes chickens so much. Anyway, the rainbow-colored bands give the rainbow trout its name. There we go, now that I got he the hook out of his mouth I can stop talking. I always talk while taking the hook out of the fish's mouth. I know that creatures that hatch out of an egg don't feel pain like animals do, but it's always hard for me to remove the hook anyway," I said.

It's hard to believe I caught two trout in less than 10 minutes. The others have just now made it down to the river. They must have had a good time talking to the old man. My trout is still in the net and I hold it up for all to see. Everyone gave me a thumb's up.

If it weren't for the short sprinkle of rain that excited the trout, I doubt I would have ever of caught him. He got caught up in the moment. He is a smart trout or he wouldn't have been so large. I'm sure he has avoided many a fly pole.

The first to approach this 20-inch trout is Kyle with Sara right behind him. "That is a awesome rainbow trout you landed Chelsea. I did not know they actually got that big. At first I thought it was a bass from a distance but I now see it is the most awesome trout my eyes have ever seen. Congratulations on the catch of the day. I know none of us can come close to this big boy. I've always heard that trophy fish in tournaments are usually caught early in the morning or very late in the evening. That is when they are most likely to feed. It's a shame we are not in a tournament, you would certainly be the winner," Kyle said.

The two lovebirds, BreAnna and Jake found a large rock they could share and had their lines in the water. Angela and Brad were looking at my trout, like what's the big deal, the catfish that Brad noodled for were much bigger. The only people that can appreciate the size of this trout are Kyle, Zack, and myself. We understand that 20 inches is really big for a trout.

Kyle began a back cast that looks like a piece of art. He made four back cast before his fly hit the water with a forward cast, which landed his fly on the water exactly where he wanted it to land. He talked to Zack and me about flies while he watched for a trout to take the bait. Kyle said, "The most popular flies are the Glow-Bug or egg fly, it looks like a floating fish egg. Also the San Juan Worm which looks like a red stick. Last but not least is the Green Inch Worm. Trout will eat minnows and worms, but trout mostly eat nymphs. You want to use a dry fly that descends lightly on the surface of the water. Trout live in a certain area of the water and eat under water bugs such as nymphs, mayflies, caddis and other bugs that hatch and become airborne, then die and the trout eat them. Dry-fly anglers like me, use a line between 5 and 7 weight and place at least 12 feet in front of them, to keep from spooking the fish. The lighter the line the softer it hits the water. You know, there is just something about fly fishing that calms me down."

Zack said, "The smartest thing you did was take advice from the old man. He knows what the trout are eating and you save a lot of time by asking what are the trout ordering off the menu today. He sure got Chelsea off to a good start today." I said, "Kyle you are right about what trout eat. Mayflies are often what trout feed on because they die after mating and fall into the river. It is a sight to see when a trout makes a splashy movement to take the mayfly in its mouth. Sometimes the trout prefers the nymphs or larval stages of flies, as well as other small aquatic creatures, such as shrimp, snails, and beetles. These are under water baits. Also, fish behave differently at different times of the day. Knowing their behavior gives you an advantage. Fish can smell so I put fish oil on all my flies after attaching them to my pole. Would you like some Kyle?"

Kyle took some fish oil and by the end of our outing, he caught four trout, I caught one more, Zack caught two and everyone else just had a good time. Kyle had difficulties ending the day. He said, "You guys watch, I know there is one more trout with my name on it. You see the shade from that overhanging tree? It is a perfect casting place for fish to hide. As Kyle's nymph drifted in the direction of the large trout we seen the white of the inside of the trout's mouth, then he took the nymph in it's mouth and Kyle pulled the pole and the fight was on. Kyle's fly rod bent down and kissed the water. We thought he lost the trout when the pole bounced back in an upright position. Suddenly it bent over again and the line was pulling out of the real with a grinding sound, it was as if the trout was in control. I grabbed the fishing net that Zack had brought and wadded out into the water in the direction of the trout. Suddenly I was under water. A drop off into deep part of the water had my feet searching for a rock or something to bounce myself back to the surface. My waders were filling up with water and my body became heavy. There is no way I can push myself to the top of the water. My lungs feel like they are about to explode. I turn lose of Zack's net and walk along the bottom of the river. I feel my head being pulled in a sidewise direction. I could feel my body going in the direction of the current. Thoughts were going through my mind that a log must have caught my hair and if I'm lucky it might just drag me to shore. I could feel myself losing concision thought.

When I woke up, Zack was breathing breath into my lungs. All my friends were rubbing my arms and legs, trying to warm them. I spit up what felt like a full glass of water. Zack was brushing my hair back and I could see his mouth moving but no sound was coming out. It is like a dream, somehow not real but at the same time crystal clear that I just drowned and Zack brought me back to life.

A shadow, on an area that seem to be partially irradiated or illuminated due to blockage of light by what seem to be the Holy Sprit, a dove. Have I died? Why is it that everyone's mouth is moving but yet I hear nothing I'm sitting up watching this bird descend towards me that is getting larger and larger. Suddenly I hear a large splash in the water, and the most beautiful chocolate colored duck sat on the water looking at me as if to say wake-up. It began quacking and going in circles. The next sound I heard was Zack saying, "Chelsea, you're going to be okay." It was as if I became aware of the voices one by one.

"I'm fine, I'm fine, I swallowed a little water, that's all. That's the most beautiful duck I've ever seen," I said. "I call him Cocoa Duck. He comes ever day about this time to say hi. I think he is a scout. When he starts his quacking and going in circles, like he is doing now, the others will soon fly in and join him. I always bring bread and throw them a few pieces. Would you like to feed him Chelsea?" Kyle said. "I would love to make this duck happy," I said.

"Chelsea, do you want to go to the hospital and get checked out," Zack said. "I'm okay, I just need to set for a moment. You know Zack; a tiny moment can change your life completely. I'm just hysterically happy to be alive right now. Kyle did you catch that monster fish?" I said. "I dropped my pole, it's somewhere down the river I guess," Kyle said. "Let's go look for it, that trout is a keeper and your fly pole and reel are worth a lot of money," I said.

I got on my feet and it was as if nothing even happened to me, other than life seem more precious to me now. We all walked down the bank of the river looking for Kyle's fly rod. BreAnna said, "Chelsea you could have died if it weren't for Zack pulling you out of the water." "I'm glad he did I prefer being on this side of the grass. Hey Kyle, there's your rod stuck between those two rocks." I said.

Kyle grabbed his rod and the fish is still on it. The fight is back on. I dropped the net when I went under water so Kyle will just have to bring him in on his own.

This time Kyle walked on the banks of the river instead of inside the water. He walked along the bank and as the fish slowed down, Kyle took up the slack in his line. Before he knew it, the fish only had around ten feet of line and was swimming along the shallow bank. Kyle just dragged him out of the water when the fish was too tired to fight any more. Turn's out it was a 25-pound stripper bass instead of a trout. That's all right, he will be tasty.

Kyle removed his polarized glasses that cut the glare from the water and his hat that must have had 50 flies hooked on it, got down on his knees and removed the hook out of the stripper mouth. He looked up at me and said, "Chelsea I'm personally going to cook this fish for you." We all got a chuckle out of that and headed for home.

Chapter 9
Bamboo

Mom and dad insisted that I see the doctor. The water that went into my lungs could have parasites so the doctor put me on antibiotics to be on the safe side.

Zack dropped by to see how I'm doing. He told me what went on after I stepped into the dark hole in the river. I thought my hair got caught on a log but it was Zack pulling my hair to drag me to the rapids, which helped him pull me from the water. Zack said, "Your waders, which are made to protect you from the cold water, filled up with water and weighed your body down. Your hair was the only thing I could grab so I did. Sorry if it hurt." I said, "No it's fine, I'm just glad you saved my life. The only thing I remember clearly is spitting up what seemed like a cup of water." Zack said, "That and then some. I breathed my breath into your lungs and pressed on your chest to get the water out. You gave all of us a scare."

I grabbed Zack's hand and headed out the back door. I wanted some fresh air to breath, just thinking that I could have died made me feel a little flushed. Bam, who was wagging her tail, greeted us and I gave her a couple of jellybeans and scratched her behind the ear. "I want to thank you for saving my life. I didn't want to make a big deal out of it in front of all our friends, but I got really scared when the waders were filling up with water. I just wasn't strong enough to pull myself up," I said. "No one would have been strong enough, not even me. I had to maneuver your body into the current of the river in order to manipulate your body into a desired position to release your waders from your body. These things get really heavy when they fill up with water. Sorry about pulling you by your hair, it was the only thing I could see at the time, and time was of the essences," Zack said.

I just smiled at Zack and he knew it was okay. We walked to the pond and sat on the bench. Bam began nudging Zack to see what was in his hand. Zack picked up a jellybean on the way out the door and opened his hand so Bam could indulge in her favorite treat, a red jellybean. Zack reached out to feel Bam's belly and said, "I believe this deer is really going to have a fawn this time. I know we all thought she was having one last year, but she just ate to many jellybeans and gained a pop belly. This time I can feel the fawn moving around in her belly. Put your hand right here Chelsea, feel that."

I can feel the fawn moving like it is coming out any minute. Zack has his hand on top of mine and I feel his energy and the energy in Bam's belly. "This is so exciting. She really has a baby in her belly. I think I shall name it Boo. That way I can call them both by saying, 'come here Bamboo' I love my Bamboo fishing pole, and I love the name Boo," I said.

Zack squeezed my hand and our eyes locked. I asked, "When you were breathing breath into my lifeless body, was it like you were kissing me?" Zack said, "I have to be honest with you, I was in such a panic all I could think about was, reviving you. I blew breath in your lungs while holding your nose closed, than I released and placed both hands, one on top of the other, on your chest, and pressed. I'm sorry to tell you, romance was the last thing on my mind."

Zack saved my life and I will forever hold him in the highest of esteem. Zack always has made me feel safe when he is around. He is the kind of man who can put food on the table no matter what, even if he has to hunt it down. He is the kind of man who puts family first, and to me this is the most important thing in life. He has charter and this is what makes him a good person. I want him to be a part of my life at whatever level he feels comfortable with. My fondness has increased for Zack immensely.

We started back to the house and Zack took my hand and I felt secure in my feelings. I gave him a quick kiss on the cheek and he gave a squeeze on my hand.

Mom and dad were sitting on the backyard furniture and waved at us when we stepped out of the woods. Dad stood up as we drew near him and shook Zack's hand and mom hugged his neck and thanked him for saving her little girl. Dad told Zack that he is part of the family and will always be in our hearts. Zack is a hero in our family even if he is trying to downplay his heroic actions at the river.

Mom asked Zack to stay for dinner. She has a chicken casserole already made and insists Zack join us. He didn't argue for he loves my mom's cooking. Zack said, "The smell of good food creates good memory's that will last a lifetime. That is why it is so important to cook for your family. Now that I'm part of the family, I say lets eat."

Zack gets along well with men and women because he has the knack to accommodate their needs with the best intentions and politeness. Zack has always said that decent behavior goes a long way. My parents need Zack to be part of their lives. After all, Zack saved their little girls life. The thought of my death sent shock waves through my parent's brains. Giving back is always the key to my parents healing. They need Zack to be part of the family to help calm their thoughts.

I asked Zack if he would mind taking me to the river tomorrow around noon so I could feed Cocoa Duck some bread. I told him about how seeing that duck coming out of the sky with the sun behind him was a very spiritual moment for me. I was unsure at the moment, if indeed I could possible be dead. When I heard the quack of Cocoa Duck, is when I realized I was alive. I've always had religion, thanks to my parent's upbringing, and I believe that religion enriches ones life, feeds one's spirit and is where peace dwells. This near death experience has given me the gift of peace. I felt it when Cocoa Duck was descending from, the sky. I had no fear and the bright light from the sun warmed my soul. I had no fear of the hereafter. It was as if I could see where God lives with uncommon clarity.

Zack said, "I'll pick you up at 11:00am and we will grab a bite to eat where Sara works. By the way, my best friend is Jesus. He has given me a free gift of love. He told me the wages of sin is death and separation from God. If you had died Chelsea, I know you would be with God, and that is true life. God's greatest gift is freedom from fear. I can see you no longer fear death. It's like you said, 'As long as were on this side of the grass were doing okay,' either side you will be okay, and never be separated from God, I see that in you."

I looked up at Zack and said, "Jeff touched my hand but you Zack, touch my soul. It's very important that I express how I feel and you always allow me to do this. I'm so crazy now I don't know how I'm able to think. I just want to have the reverberating sound of Cocoa Duck quacking."

It is evening and Cloie has sent me an E-Mail requesting a live chat over the computer. Mom told her of the events at the river and Cloie felt an urgent need to talk to me. The next E-Mail was from Jeff. Yes the guy who asked me to leave him alone because he has no idea as to who I'm. Cloie requested I contact her an hour from now so I'm going to read Jeff's E-mail now. He wrote, "Tragedy in a family is sometimes called a crucible or a sever trial. When this comes into a family, the members take it out on each other unless they request outside help to get through the rough times. This is necessary in order to heal. The death of a child, or in my case the death of a child's mind temporarily, is a good example. Guilt and blame causes anger, and one must let lose of the anger. You are the outside help that my family needed, and I thank you for that help. Matt contacted me and told me about your near death experience. It sounds to me like you have more work to do on earth before you enter the Kingdom of Heaven. You truly are one of God's angels on earth."

I had to stop and caught my breath as I finished reading Jeff's E-Mail. I thought to myself, 'Hey dial it back will you,' all this time you say you have no idea who I'm and now you are sending me E-mail's like you've known me all your life. I feel like a yo yo on the end of a string right now, fixing to be all wound up in Jeff again. My thoughts are going wild.

As I click on the respond button, Jeff is sending me a live feed and there we are face to face. "You look well Chelsea, even after what all you have been through," Jeff said. "I just finished reading your mail and I appreciate your words. I'm doing fine as you can see," I said. "Yes you look lovely as always. My memory is improving daily now. I have revisited the E-mail's we exchanged before the accident, and I now remember who you are. I see we had a special relationship and I hope to regain those feelings, in the near future. Right now it is like I'm in a dream state, half awake and half asleep. I know it is real because it is in writing, but it is still fussy. By the way, Matt called me and he and Cloie will be in Oklahoma on April third. Ed is talking about the two of us driving down to see them, and your family, and of course you."

We talked for another half hour but we were like strangers compared to our relationship in Florida. Jeff is keeping me at a distance and I'm okay with this. It is so much better than Jeff not wanting me to even talk to him. I will let him come back to me at his speed. I'm excited to see him and Ed but

I'm not going to get all pumped up about a relationship like we once had. I'm just going to enjoy him.

Cloie answered my live chat right away. "Little sister you gave us all a scare. Are you okay?" Cloie said. "Yes I'm just fine. It is a real eye opener to know I could have drowned and you would be attending my funeral in a couple of days. I'm a pretty good kid but now I think more attention to God is in order. Jeff talked to me just an hour ago and he and Ed are coming down when you and Matt come home this next time. He is starting to remember who Chelsea is and that is exciting," I said. "Yes we will be there before you know it. Got to go now but just wanted to say 'stay safe,' and hope Jeff is the way you remembered him in Florida. Love you," Cloie said.

Zack is right on time, Today is our day and I refuse to mention that I talked to Jeff last night. I feel closer to Zack than ever before. After all he saved my life.

When we walked into the restaurant, all my friends were their and waving us over to the table. BreAnna and Jake insisted that I sit between them. Zack nodded his head in acceptance and he sat between Sara and Kyle. Everyone talked about what a scare I gave him or her, and insisted I be more careful in the future.

It is always good to see my friends, and I gave each of them a hug. It's time to go because Cocoa Duck arrives at noon and I want to be there when he drops from the sky.

We are five minutes early and have plenty of bread for all the ducks that visit this river today. Zack said, "This is the spot where I got you to shore. That is the rapid that helped me bring you out of the deep water. That is the direction that Cocoa Duck came in from and there he is, right on time."

He dropped from the sky with the same grace that he did yesterday. He is beautiful, just like the first time I seen him. He immediately began quacking and going in circles. I laughed at the enthusiasm at which he called in all his friends. They all dropped from the sky around Cocoa Duck and he was in heaven. We tossed one slice of bread at a time until the loaf was gone. They had a good meal and we had fun feeding them. Next it is time to see the old man. I looked up the bluff and seen a shimmer of the window glass. "Let's go see if he is home," I said.

When we made it to the top of the bluff and looked in the window, the beautiful flies are a sight to see once again but the old man is nowhere in sight. Zack said, "Let's go to his son's house. It's not that much further. By the way, the old man's name is Mr. Hunter."

"I see you are okay little girl. By the time I made it down the bluff, all of you were gone," said Mr. Hunter. "Oh, does that mean you seen what happened to me?" I said. "Yes little one, I watched as your friend pulled you into the rapids, so they could help move you to safety. You must always wear a tube filled with air if you plan to walk into water's where you can't see the bottom of the stream," said Mr. Hunter. "I got caught up in the moment. I didn't want that fish to get away," I said.

The old man got us something to drink and we talked for near an hour. He had some good fish stories but none toped mine. Could be because it happened to me.

When we arrived back to my house I gave Zack a hug and thanked him for a wonderful day. I'm tired and in need of a nap. The medicine the doctor gave me has that effect on me.

It's been two weeks since my near drowning and I'm back 100% to my old self. Spring break starts this week and Cloie and Matt will be here tomorrow, in the USA that is. They plan to stay the first day with Matt's family and then drive down the next day to be with our family. I'm in charge of getting their room ready and the whole thing is so exciting. The last time Matt slept in our house he was alone, this time he will share with his wife Cloie.

Today is April first and I'm trying to think of something

good to pull on my parents for April fool's day, when my mother knocked on my bedroom door. I asked her to come in. "Chelsea we have a new addition to the family, Bam has a little one now," Mother said. "Yea right, this year you got me first. April fool's day," I said. "No really come look," mom said.

I followed her out the door and in the middle of a large pile of leaves lay this beautiful fawn with white spots on it's backside. It looked exactly like Bam when she was given to me. Boo blended in with the leaves so good that if mom hadn't pointed her out to me I would have walked right past her. I scratched Bam on the back of her head and said, "Good job."

Chapter 10
Cloie and Matt Return

After a couple of hours Boo is up and running around like she owned the place. This is the most beautiful thing I've ever seen. Bam is a great mother and has taken Boo around to introduce her to each of us. It's as if Boo's eyes are bigger than her head. That's an exaggeration but she does have really big eyes, and they seem to get bigger when we scratch behind her ear.

It's three days later and Cloie and Matt are pulling into the driveway with Ed and Jeff right behind them. Cloie jumped out of the car and grabbed us for a group hug. "I've missed you something awful," Cloie said. Matt first, then Ed and last Jeff followed with warm welcomes. Everyone is talking about the flight from Russia and the drive from Texas except Jeff. Jeff and myself are just staring at each other's face to see how we are going to relate.

Jeff's eyes are warm but when he hugged me it was an empty feeling. Kind of like we are still strangers physically but have a shared experience with the near death episodes. Mentally we understand what few people have experienced, near death.

Ed and Jeff left to make reservations at a Hotel. We offered them a place to stay but they insisted on getting their own place. They assured us they would be back in time for dinner. I think Jeff still has trouble being around a lot of people for long periods of time.

"Cloie, Matt, I've got something to show you two. Just follow me. This is the new addition to the family, her name is Boo. She was born April the first and she is every bit as sweet as Bam was when she was a baby. Watch her eyes get bigger when I scratch her behind the ears," I said. "Chelsea, she is adorable. She looks identical to Bam the first time I saw Bam. I love the name. What made you think of Boo," Cloie said. "You know my bamboo fly rod that Grandpa gave me, that's where the idea originated. After swallowing that water, when I went fishing with the Bamboo pole, it seems to be on my mind. Besides, when I call them both all I have to say is 'Bamboo, come here.' I always look for the easy way to do things," I said.

Matt gave Bam and Boo a scratch behind their ears and we headed for the pond. It's to early in the year to swim but it is a beautiful place to just sit and enjoy nature. The Red Bud trees are in full bloom and truly are a sight to see. The water is clear and along the bank are crawdads with pinchers as long as my fingers. Cloie pointed and said, "Those guys will make good fish bait." I nodded in agreement.

We could hear a voice that none of us could recognize and Cloie said, "Let's go check it out, I'm curious as to who dad is talking to."

When dad caught sight of us he called us over. "This is our local vet Matt. The family donates enough money to fix either two dogs or two cats or one of each every year so they cannot reproduce unwanted offspring's. We believe the solution to unwanted pets, that either starve or get put to sleep, is to prevent pets from reproducing unwanted offspring's. We give our donation every April to this vet so some young kid can have a pet that won't become a problem. We see no need to pay some organization our hard earned money to do paper work, or go around looking for unwanted pets to put to sleep. We believe in getting to the root cause, which is preventing any pets from ever being born that are unwanted. This vet fixes the problem and finds the dogs and cats a home with no charge to the new owners. You see, no money is wasted, the only one who get's paid is the one who get's the job done, the vet. When Bam is done nursing Boo, this fine gentleman will be fixing the both of them. Two deer's is all this family needs," dad said.

"Your dad has the right idea, if more people took a proactive approach to get the money to the people who actually can perform the surgery to prevent unwanted pet's, the problem would go away. God put pets on earth for people to enjoy. Not everyone has enough money for the surgery, but thanks to people like your dad, who puts the money right in my hand, I've made two families very happy this year. Here are the pictures of the two families with the new pets that, thanks to your dad, won't reproduce unwanted offspring's. I always give him a picture so he knows for sure where his hard earned money goes." said the vet.

"I have three places that I always donate money to, the first is our church second is the orphanage and third is to this fine young vet. This year I'm donating money for Chelsea to get her deer's fixed, it's a good cause," dad said.

"I have no objections, one baby is enough for Bam. I thank you dad for thinking of your daughter. After all we can't have twenty deer's all wanting jelly beans," I said.

Mom called me to the phone and Ed was on the line, "Chelsea, I'm sorry to tell you that Jeff has had a very eventful day and tonight we are just staying in. I hope you don't mind. We think we will make it out tomorrow around noon, if that's okay with you and your family." "Sure I understand, Jeff was very quite today, I could tell it was a little much for him still," I said. "Yes Chelsea it was a lot for him. You know he is a strong as a bull until he gets emotionally upset, even if it is a good emotionally upset, he becomes as weak as a kitten behind it," Ed said. "See you tomorrow," I said.

Noon could not come to soon enough for me. I stayed up half the night trying to figure out just what is going on in Jeff's head. Is he ever going to feel about me like he once did, or are we going to just be friends with shared experiences? Does he feel quilt because he asked that I stop contacting him? I prayed all night for the answer and what came into my mind is, 'accept whatever God's plan is,' it's that simple.

As I watched Ed and Jeff pull into the driveway my heart skipped a beat. They got out of the car and were walking around my Mustang. As I walked up to them I asked, "Would you two like to go for a ride." "Oh Chelsea, good morning, yes we would love to go for a ride. Jeff wants to go to the river where you were fishing," Ed said. "What you mean to say is 'where I almost drowned,' and lost my life." I said.

Jeff looked at me and nodded his head in agreement with what I had said. I offered to drive my car and they both agreed that it would be nice to go for a spin in the Mustang. As we pulled into the parking place near the river, Jeff commented, "This whole area that you live in is breathtaking. You must be happy living amongst all this beauty." "Absolutely, it is like living in paradise," I said.

Jeff wanted to see the spot where I swallowed water. When I pointed to the only still water in the river, Jeff asked me to tell him what was going on in my head while it was happening. I replied, "It was like a nightmare, not really happening to me. As I started going down I held my breath and tried to swim to the surface. My body was so heavy with water in my waiters that no matter how hard I tried to surface, I just went down. It was as if everything was in slow motion, time was beginning to stand still, I was not sure if I was dead or alive. All I could think is I need to survive because I have a lot left to do in this world."

Jeff gave me a hug. He let me know that it is good to talk about bad experiences because it helps you deal with it. "You can focus on your heartbeat as a sound sensation. Ask yourself who am I, what do I want? Then let yourself experience gratitude for something that someone did nice for you. Try to experience love with your thoughts and this will lead to emotional healing," Jeff said.

Jeff has so much insight into people's emotions. He sees into my mind. I've acted like this event is no big deal, but Jeff see's I'm an emotional wreck behind it. This ability to be sensitive to one's needs is part of what is so attractive about Jeff to me. He is so right about the need to focus on the good things like gratitude, which I feel for Zack for saving my life. When Jeff said to try and experience love with my thoughts, did he mean the love I've felt for him before his accident? I don't dare ask him if that is what he meant. If I'm wrong he might shut me out again. I'm just going to roll with what he says and let him be the aggressor.

Things became very quite when suddenly Ed broke the silence and said, "Is that Mr. Hunters house in the side of the bluff. It's well hidden and I would never have noticed it if you hadn't mentioned it to me earlier. Do you think we could give him a visit." "Sure if you don't mind the long walk up the side of the bluff. By the time we make it to his shop you will be calling this a mountain," I said.

As we started our journey up the bluff Ed and Jeff keep talking about how dense the foliage is and it's a good thing they have me as their guide for they are sure they would have turned around and started back down by now. The trail wines around to the point that you feel like you are going in circles.

When I returned with Mr. Hunter and introduced him to Jeff first, than Ed, Mr. Hunter shook their hands, but held on to Ed's hand and said, "Your trails are over, you have a new life, make the most of it." We all looked at each other, like this truly is a strange moment.

The old man unlocked the door to his shop and as we entered

the sun broke through the clouds and illumined the hundreds of flies on the three walls. Ed said, "This is an awesome sight. I've never seen such a richly varied colorfulness in one room. How much do you need for that large fly with the yellow wings and green body?" Mr. Hunter removed it from the wall and handed it to Ed, and said, "I give you this fly and hope you enjoy eating the large mouth bass you will catch with it."

Ed thanked the old man for the fly and the old man took us to the window and said, "Chelsea, your friend is about to arrive." About that time we watched as Cocoa Duck came out of the sky, gliding down to the very spot where I went under the water. It is the only spot on the river where the current isn't pushing water down stream, and Cocoa Duck begins swimming in circles just like the first time I seen him.

As we were driving back to my house, Ed said, "You know when the old man shook my hand and said, 'Your trials are over,' I felt a spiritual energy pass between us. Do you think he could see something that is beyond normal." "I think he can see that your head looks like it wore out two bodies. That would be because of all the drugs you have done. We can see your eyes are clear and look normal so you have changed your life. Things have to get better when you quit poisoning yourself," Jeff said. They both were laughing out loud and before I knew it I was laughing to. They have a dark but honest sense of humor. "Since I quit doing drugs, I have developed a personal relationship with God. I think the old man sensed that. I read the Bible every day now and God gives me the ability to understand what the messages he gives are about for me. What I have learned is that it goes against your divine nature to sin, and that sin brings unhappiness. To me drugs are a sin, and when you sin you make Satan powerful because he can kill your soul. Fear yourself if you are sinning for you are killing your soul. I don't want to be the one who just doesn't get it. I will love myself, and love changes a person from where they are to where they should be. God is now the foundation of my life. God's church is nothing but the foundation that I now live my life on," Ed said.

"Listening to you I feel like I'm in church right now. I think your calling could be a preacher," I said. "Yes little sister, I could be a preacher, and if I were my message to you would be 'The greatest gift you can give yourself is everlasting life in heaven,' because if you keep making mistakes like dropping off in deep holes of water with waders on, your not going to last here on earth much longer. Little brother that goes for you also. With my tack record for messing up you better double-check anything to do with me, like helmets. I think I would spend a little more money on a trusted brand to protect your head if you plan to play any more football," Ed said.

We could not help but laugh at the way Ed puts things. Jeff said, "I've been meaning to talk to you Chelsea about being more careful. Neither one of us will ever make it to centenarian's if were not a little more careful. I know we talked about how when we walk into a grocery store that we look at it like we are walking into a pharmacy full of good things to keep our bodies healthy, but one careless mistake can mess up all those good things we do for our bodies."

"Well here's Miss Sunshine driving the car and here's Mr. Rain Cloud in the back seat dishing out orders. Right now my soul is on fire and I have one last thing to say to the both of you, 'Fear not them who kill the body but not the soul,' Matthue 10," said Ed.

"You are so right Ed, the soul is the only thing that lives with God forever. However, I have a lot of good to do here on earth yet and I need this body to fulfill my task. Besides, Jeff and myself made a pack to live healthy lives until we are 100 years old," I said.

When we finally made it to the house, Cloie invited us to

set at the table to listen to some of the stories they were telling about Russia. Matt was in the middle of a story about churches. He was telling how Russia has churches on the river. A large boat goes from one town to another and docks so people can go to church that live in the small towns.

Next Cloie told a story about ice water swimming. Cloie said, "In Russia you have this group of people who go ice water swimming. They say at first the water is freezing your body, than you become warm. They say that ice swimming brings you joy and makes you feel kind."

I so enjoyed everyone for the couple of days I was able to spend with them before they headed back, Cloie and Matt to Russia, and Ed and Jeff to Texas. I wish they could all have stayed longer. Jeff seemed warm and responsive most of the time but had a tendency to slip back into his shell.

I left Jeff with the word, 'encroaching,' for a big word to add to his vocabulary. The word encroaching means to intrude gradually on the rights or possessions of another. He looked at me like, 'What are you talking about.' This is how Jeff is now. He goes in and out. Hopefully he will want to talk to me a lot. I had the best time with him, even though he was very guarded with me.

Chapter 11

Prom

The senior Prom is on every senior's mind this month. Will any one ask me to the Prom? Will I ask anyone to go to the Prom? If you don't have a steady boyfriend, or if you're a guy, a steady girlfriend, these are the questions going through your mind.

At the lunch table everyone was talking about Prom night. The Prom dinner is being held at a restaurant on the banks of Lake Tenkiller. Many of the already couples like BreAnna and Jake, Angela and Brad, Sara and Kyle are talking about taking pictures on a certain rock with the lake in the background. Kyle goes to a different school than we do, but Sara has asked him to be her date, and he accepted. Zack made a comment about how he would be wearing a tie to match the dress of the lady he would be escorting to the Prom. My heart fell to my feet when he said that. Had Zack asked someone to the Prom and I'm the last to find out about it? Does this mean that I might be sitting home on Prom night? I could not stand the suspense any longer; I had to ask Zack who was he taking to the Prom. He just looked at me and said, "That's a no-brainer. You Chelsea will be my date, of coarse. I'm hoping you will wear that turquoise dress you wore to Cloie's wedding, the one that I seen in the pictures." I said, "Are you taking me for granted. You did not even ask me to go to the Prom. What if someone else already asked me to go? Then what will you do?" I said.

Zack immediately got out of his chair, dropped down on one knee and said, "Chelsea my darling girl, may I escort you to the Prom? Before you answer this, last weekend I purchased the perfect tie to match your dress." Everyone at the table waited for my response. I could feel my face turning red as I looked around the cafeteria, which had gone completely silent. Everyone's eyes were upon my lips now waiting in anticipation of my answer. I responded, "Of course my night in shinning armor, who saved this danzel in distress. Your tie will go perfect with my dress, I'm sure of that." The whole cafeteria stood up and clapped as if they had just watched great performance.

I had to challenge Zack, can't just let him take me for granted. It put a little spark in our relationship. Zack became more aware of my insecurities today.

When Zack knocked on the door, I asked my mom, "Do I look okay?" Her response was, "You truly are lovely tonight. Now answer that door." When I opened the front door, Zack stood on the porch dressed in a white tux with long tails, a turquoise tie that matched my dress perfect and a large white corsage that he slipped on my wrist and then kissed me on my cheek. I smelled the carnation corsage and my senses were filled with the fragrance of the soft peddles of the real carnation. Zack knows I'm not into the fake flowers some guys give their girlfriends. I looked up at Zack and said, "You are very handsome. Thank you for the carnation corsage. I love the touch of a cool soft petal of a real flower." Zack said, "Chelsea you look stunning. I'm glad you are wearing the necklaces Cloie gave you. It speaks volumes. Shall we go now?" I said, "As soon as I pin your boutonniere on your jacket. It matches my necklace, white and turquoise. Do you like it?" Zack said, "I love it." Zack offered me his arm and I slid mine into his and off we went.

The gang of young future centenarians are waiting at the door for our arrival. Everyone looks stunting, strikingly attractive in appearance, with formal clothes, shinny shoes, and hair fixed perfect. BraAnna called out, "Over here, we want to all sit together." Zack said, "We better get in their if we are to find a table big enough for all of us." The guys pulled two tables together and we sat down. The two choices of meat were steak and chicken. There is an impressive display of vegetables such as asparagus with succulent young shoots that look very edible. Baked potatoes with butter, sour cream, and chives. Salad with purple cabbage, shredded carrot's and small round red tomatos. Wheat rolls, white rolls with cheese topping and flat bread, cut into four pieces. Needless to say dinner is delicious. Now we are off to the Ballroom. The ten-peace band is already playing music and they are really good. All of the tables are covered with cloth and a lit candle sits in the center of each table.

Excitement is in the air as we take our places at the tables. BreAnna is sitting next to me and said, "The air is filled with beauty and goodness tonight." I responded, "Indeed it is."

Ballroom type music is now playing and we get in a circle, guys on the outside and girls on the inside. The guys go around in the opposite direction of the girls and at certain time's in the music, both stop and hook each others arm together and spin around. That way each of us gets to dance in a circle with each other's partner. It makes the girls feel like English royalist and the guy's feel like English gentlemen. It gave each of us a personal moment with our very good friends. It was nice.

As the night went on the band got warmed up, and they just got better and better. Most of the girls by now have shucked their high heels. If you don't wear them a lot, they won't be broke in and can cause a lot of pain. Some of the girls, who pined their hair on top of their heads, have let it down and are having the time of their lives. We just have a great group of seniors who know how to have good clean fun.

The last dance of the night is a slow dance. The band introduced each member of the band, and we all hupped and hollered to show our appreciation, for his or her talent. Without stopping the music they broke into what they said was their favorite slow song and they hope we like it as well. The song is Hey Jude by the Beatles. My parents play this song a lot so it is familiar to me and I do love it.

The senior Prom was a perfect evening. I smell my carnation while looking at the stars. Zack said, "Look Chelsea, a falling star, or a shooting star, whatever you want to call it." I said, "Yes I see it. Looks like a comet, it's so big. Where do you think they go after the light goes out? Do they evaporate, or are they a rock floating around in space now? Hope it doesn't hit earth."

I could feel Zack looking at me and when I turned to face him he said, "Chelsea, I'm so glad to know you. This night will always hold a special place in my heart. You were the prettiest girl at the Prom." Zack definitely got my attention; it was like a breath of fresh air and before I knew it my mouth was drawing closer and closer to Zack's until I could feel his breath on my face. I swallowed the lump in my throat and kissed him. At first the kiss was sweet just like the first time I kissed Zack but the longer our lips were together the stronger the feelings became until the sweetness was turning to passion. It was as if I was being swallowed up in passion, and than Zack pulled back and the feelings vanished as quickly as they began.

Zack said, "We just exchanged some mighty powerful feelings. We better watch ourselves. We obviously have an attraction, that is if you felt what I felt." I said, "I did, I did." Zack jumped out of the car, opened my door and walked me to the door. He gave me a kiss on the cheek and said, "I really enjoyed this day, good night."

When I went into the house, mom and dad were watching TV; I floated around the house like I could hear the ballroom music in my head. Mom said, "You look like you had a good time tonight." I said, "Mother, Dad, it would be a wonderful world if every day were Prom day. I feel like a princess, yes like royalty."

I put my carnation corsage under my mom's nose and she took a smell and said, "That is heavenly." I put it under my nose once more and began floating around the room again, like I was ballroom dancing.

Chapter 12

Graduation

I'm truly going to miss my high school days. All the teens will have special memories for me, the way they matured, the way they ware their hair, the style of clothing they chose, the sporting events they participated in, and the lunch room, filled with hungry teens. It's the whole package that I will be missing.

Jake is giving the farewell speech and he started with, "Let's begin with a moment of silence and thank all those who have had a part in each of us who are graduating from high school on this wonderful evening. It could be your mother and father who got you up in the morning and fixed you a healthy breakfast so you could do your work in school. Or the teacher, who explained things until it sunk in. Or a friend, who studied with you after school hours, that improve your grades. Or God, who gave you the greatest book ever written to live your life by, the Bible. I now ask you to open your heart and give thanks.

Going forward in your endeavors, I want each and every one of you to continue to read, read, read. It's okay to read the same book over and over if you really like it. You will be surprised that each time you read it; something will get your attention.

I want each of you to think about where you want to wind up in life. Set goals and think about them all the time. Thinking is very powerful. Continue to reinvent yourself.

This way you will always have talents. I'm an inventor and my next invention will be with mirrors capturing sunlight and carrying it under the floors of a house in tubes, to warm it. I continue to think of things that will make our earth a better place to live. I'm challenging you to do the same.

The best advice I can share with you is don't be in a hurry to find your mate in life, they will come along eventually. Don't settle just to say you have someone. Wait for the right person. You must like the person you wind up with because your children could have their personality. Your stuck with your children, for a lifetime, they will always be in your life. They are your family. If you like the person you marry, the chances of keeping your family together are in your favor. You don't want to become a statistic of the divorced people in this new age and time. Love yourself and love your family. Keep your body strong with exercise and healthy foods.

The last advice I have to give you is to protect your freedom with your power of the vote. Yes, all of you are very powerful, so flex your muscles at the voting poles.

If you seek advice, go to an elder who has a proven record. In other words, if you were looking for advice on relationships of a boyfriend, girlfriend nature, you wouldn't seek out someone who had been divorced ten times. Now would you? You would look for a couple celebrating their 50th wedding anniversary. Be smart about the people you chose to mentor you.

For me, the most important thing in my life is being in good standing with God. Everything else will fall in place because my faith will be in God and he will guide me. God speaks to me through the Bible. All the answers to my questions are in this Book. It is the greatest gift every, and I read it every day. That's all I have to say."

The whole auditorium is on there feet clapping their hands. We could hear BreAnna over everyone's voice saying, "That my Jake."

Eyes were darting in every direction from our classmates, knowing that some of these people we would never see again in our lives. Others we would see at the five-year class reunion. It is an empty feeling knowing this. I'm just soaking it all in and I'm grateful to have been a part of such a great class.

Jake stepped away from the podium and than stepped right back up. "I know I said that's all, but I would like to say a couple of more things about family. You must give your children guidance. They can make your life heaven or hell. Keep this in the back of your mind at all times. If a little guidance will keep them from being a drug addict, or a bad man who winds up in jail, or a member of a gang that terrorize society, wouldn't it be worth the time spent trying to teach them how to handle life. If you see early on that you are unable to reach your children, than get outside help. Seek help in your church or the big brother, big sister organization. Maybe your parents can help, the grandparents of your child. What I'm trying to say is, don't wait until things are out of hand to act. Get help.

I want to share a story with you about a little fellow who's parents both worked two jobs to provide the family shelter, clothing, and food on the table. They were living in a neighborhood that cost every dime they made to live in. A small home with more time for the family would have been a much better choice for all concerned. The boy's name is Joe. One day when I was walking home from school, Joe approached me and asked if I wanted to buy some drugs. At the time I was 14 years old and Joe was only 12 years old. I said to him, 'Let me see what you got.' Joe reached into his pocket and pulled out a bag that had some white little rock like things in it. I asked him what they were and he shrugged his shoulders and said he forgot what they are called, but they will make you feel real good. Than I asked him where he got them and he said, "I can't tell you that, I might get hurt if I tell you whom he is." I didn't push the issue as to who gave him the drugs but I did begin to give him some guidance. I asked Joe what would happen to him if the police were to see him trying to sell these drugs. Joe responded with great enthusiasm, "They can't do anything to me, I'm only 12 years old." What if your parents found out about this thing you are doing. Joe said, "They are to busy to worry about what I do. Most of the time they don't even talk to me." I told Joe that if he continued doing what he's doing he would be hurting a lot of people. He would be responsible for the ruin of their lives. Some may even die because he sold them drugs. I asked him how would he explain his actions to God. Joe looked down in shame and told me he would return the drugs to the person he got them from. He let me know he never thought about messing up anyone's life, and if he did cause someone to die, that God would not like that.

I became a mentor for Joe and it is one of the most gratifying experiences of my life. Joe would come by my house and help out with some of my experiments. Joe is very intelligent and doing well in school and just started working on a part time job after school hours for a automobile repair shop. If Joe had not run into me that day, he very well could have been in prison or could have joined a gang. He thanks me on a regular basis for giving him guidance when he needed it the most. What Joe will never know, is how much of a difference he has made for me. I try to tell him how helping him filled my heart with pride, and he helped me in life just as much as I helped him. Instead of calling him Joe, I refer to him as little brother.

Life should not always be about you. Great satisfaction can be achieved through helping others get on the right track. If you contribute to the betterment of mankind you will receive satisfaction. Just think what a wonderful world we all would have if all the blessed people gave the underprivileged the opportunity to feel they are wanted. If we showed we care enough to take time out of our busy day to offer some guidance to a young person we see stumbling in the wrong direction. I say to you, go out into the big world of ours and make a difference in someone's life that is not as fortunate as you. Give of yourself; give guidance to those who need you. Thank you, and have a wonderful life. Go out and find your Joe." Once again all were on their feet with applause, only this time it is louder and longer.

After Jake gave his speech we all threw our hats in the air in celebration of our accomplishment of 12 years of intense studying. We are all beaming with pride and we should be. We are all proud of ourselves because we could have been a statistic of just another drop out because we got boarded, or we just weren't trying hard enough to make good grades. The drop out rate of teen's is growing ever year. Some who drop out come from bad home situations that demanded they drop out and get a job just to put food on the table. We never know just what the situation of a dropout is, we don't judge. We are blessed to have graduated and give thanks to God for our education this day.

Excitement is filling the air at the thought that soon we will be going to college and choosing a career to support our future families. Everyone is tossing around their ideas of what their future looks like to them. Jake got a full scholarship because his grades in science were outstanding. Jake is always full of ideas to improve how things are done, to save the world from greenhouse gasses. I know he will excel at whatever he chooses as a career. BreAnna also got a scholarship; hers is for Basketball. This is great because she wants to be a coach someday. Zack's parents are sending him to medical school to become a surgeon. Zack also wants to become a politician to protect people's rights. He plans to do both. First he will be a surgeon to get the first half of his life in order, buy a home raise a family, and the second half of his life will be in politics. Zack sets goals in life and that is what drives him. He can make his parents happy by becoming a surgeon and helping the sick, and when he is older, pursue his passion as a politician. Most politicians have a little age on them before they are considered knowledgeable of the laws and methods used by politicians.

Brad, Angela and Sara are joining the Peace Core. This way their college is paid for depending on how many months they can contribute. For each tour of duty they receive around $5,000 that goes toward their education. They may even get credit on their transcript for out of country tours, depending on where they attend college. In the Peace Core they will be building houses, digging wells for water, and educating the young in countries that are experiencing poverty. All love the idea of spreading the word of God. Just the thought of it brings all three of them joy.

Angela's grandparents are living on a fixed income and cannot afford to pay for college. This is why she is going to join the Peace Core. Brad's grades won't get him any scholarships and his family lives on a modest income and also cannot afford college tuition and books. Sara could make great grades but she missed too much school to get the grades necessary for a scholarship. She will do great in the Peace Core as a leader because she has the personality of a leader.

Angela is deeply devoted to touching as many disturbed souls as possible. She plans to work with abused women and drug addicts as a counselor when she graduates from college. Angela feels a calling to help these troubled souls because she has seen first hand what drugs can do to a person. Angela's mother became addicted to drugs and at the time of her mothers addiction Angela was to young and did not have the knowledge to help her mother or herself. With an education she hopes to reach others and bring them out of despair and darkness that drugs lead to in the end. You see in the beginning drugs help take away problems in a false way. Drugs disguise, change the manner or appearance of in order to prevent recognition, or in plan English, they just hide the problem which keeps coming back when the victim is not high. The disguise is temporary and the problem is still there. One has to face the problem before it goes away. Everything gets worse when they become addicts. The end result of an addict is they lose their job, than their family then their life if they don't get help. Angela wants to arm herself with the knowledge to fight addiction for others through her education. She hopes to make a difference in the troubled souls life on earth.

Brad on the other hand plans to become a DEA agent to prevent distribution of illegal drugs, which he sees as the root cause of most drug addicts today. Availability makes it easy to do the wrong thing. Alcoholic beverages are legal and lead to addiction in some cases, however most people who consume alcoholic beverages do so in celebration. Those who consume alcoholic beverages to disguise a problem are at risk of becoming one who suffers from alcoholism. Alcoholic beverages are legal and only 10% who drink them ever become alcoholics, about the same amount of people become addicts to pills. Both have underlying problems that cause the addiction. Brad understands this and hopes to prevent the availability of dangerous drug's getting into the hands of people who are experiencing a crisis situation. The illegal drugs today can make an addict out of a person with just one use. That is scary. Our youth today will try drugs just to see what they will do out of curiosity, something novel or extraordinary that arouses their interest, and they just want to see what the drug will do. If Brad can keep these drugs from ever reaching our schools, he will be successful as a DEA agent in his heart. This is his passion and it's a good one. When kids get older they realize the danger and are less likely to put this poison in their precious bodies.

Sara, with all her personality, wants to make a difference in the homeless people's lives. Sara intends to do this by becoming a social worker. She is fully aware that some people are perfectly happy being homeless and it is their choice to live in a tent or in the streets of the city. Some just don't want any responsibility of a job or paying for a house, or raising children. Others were at one time productive citizens who lost their job, or people who had high stress jobs and had breakdowns, and as a result, he or she, felt more comfortable living on the street as a homeless person. Many of the mentally ill wind-up as homeless people because no one wants them living in their home, not even their family. Sad as that sounds, it is a fact, that many mentally ill are homeless.

My plan for the future is to apply for grants for my education to become a teacher. The age group, that interests me most, is the 15 year olds. This is the age that needs the most guidance in my opinion. All kinds of hormones are rushing through the body at age 15 and this is when students need the most guidance. I had my sister to talk to, and this is what saved me during this dangerous year of 15. Not everyone has someone to give guidance. I want to be there to help students during their transformation of becoming aware of adult feelings they have while still being children. I personally know the issues that 15 year olds are faced with, and if they know what is coming their direction, and have been informed about how to handle it, the better the outcome.

The teen brain is maturing in reasoning and judgment, and develops at a rapid speed. Our youth has a tendency to use poor judgment when it comes to substances that damage their brains. They refuse to acknowledge the results of substance that impair judgment and lead to addiction or early sex until it's to late, or have an accident that could kill them or their friends. Instead of realizing that they are putting their brain development at risk, they will try drugs just to look cool. They ignore the negative consequences, including addiction. If I can offer education programs that deal with prevention or delaying substance use, teens will become mature enough to realize the devastating effects of tobacco, alcohol, meth, or cocaine.

I see the problem as being that teachers are failing to act on what they see before their very eyes. Substance use should be looked at as preventable. Addiction is a disease that is treatable and the earlier it is caught the better the results. Teachers turning their heads and ignoring what is before their very eyes is condoning teen's behavior.

I plan to show teens the effect of what they think is cool, as being devastating to their health. If they see a pair of lungs damaged by tobacco with black spots, or a heart that exploded because of cocaine use they may think twice before lighting up or snorting. A package of tobacco cost five dollars and most addicted people buy two packs a day. That's $300 a month and $3600 a year going up in smoke. You can have a lot of fun on that much money. I don't know how much cocaine cost or how often it is used, but I hear it is even more expensive than tobacco. Also showing a meth addict that looks 60 years old, but is only 30 years old, doesn't look so cool either.

The power to say no to the pusher of drugs is the answer for most teens. I hope to give them the power they need. The result of addiction is destruction of God's temple and even death.

It's important to me to make learning fun. If these young people are having fun by competing with each other, the drop out rate will decrease. It would hurt my soul to have a student drop out of school on my watch. I would feel like a failure. If I see a struggling student having problems learning a lesson I will pair them up with a student that has a clear understanding of the subject. By pulling each student up by their bootstraps, we save them and ourselves. Hopefully they become a productive member of society instead of a statistic of uneducated entitlement person and a burden on society. The more education one attains the better chance of getting a job that they can support a family with. If a student drops out at 15 years of age the chances go up for joining a gang, stealing to survive because it's much harder to get a job, or working in a hard labor job. Let's hope they can get a hard labor job, we will all be safe that way. I have pearls of wisdom to share with my future student's; we are all in this thing called life together, so lets help one another be all we can be.

Jake is going to be a scientist that will make greenhouse gases a thing of the past. He is passionate about changing the destructive nature of mankind on the environment. He is currently working on a filter to capture emissions before they ever enter the atmosphere. His mind is always coming up with better ways to do things, and I know he will be successful at whatever he does in the scientific world.

My parents found me among all the graduating students and we had a group hug. Dad said, "My little Songbird, I'm so proud of you. Today I'm a success. Both of my girls have graduated from high school. I've done my part now you do your part by going to college." I grabbed him and kissed his cheek. Mom said, "Little Songbird, you make me proud as well." I grabbed my mom and kissed her cheek and said, "Thank you mom for getting me up every morning so I could get to school on time. If it weren't for you I don't know if I would have graduated today."

I have the best parents, not everyone can say that about their parents. They told me to enjoy the rest of the evening and blew me kisses as they left.

Everyone is meeting up at Sara's house to party down.

We are all excited about the new endeavors we are about to embark upon. There is excitement as well as fear of the unknown in the air. We will all be going our separate ways after summer is over.

Sara hugged my neck when I got out of Zack's truck and then hugged Zack when he got out. She said, "I love you guys, my heart is racing at the thought that we are all going our separate ways come September. The racing is from fear of missing you guys. Just because Angela and Brad are also joining the Peace Core, it doesn't mean we will be together. We may all three be overseas, only in different countries. I hope I'm doing the right thing." I said, "Don't worry, we will talk on the phone all the time, skyping is the greatest new technologies that makes it like your right in front of each other, face to face. We will all be fine, we have God on our side. Just talk to Him if you get lonely. Besides, I've never seen you lonely, you have the gift of gab." Sara said, "Thanks Chelsea, I feel better already."

Sara's Base stereo is blasting and I feel the mood of the music in my feet. The garage door is up and a table with refreshments looks great right now. I poured up a glass of lemonade and Zack said, "I'll have the same." Angela and Brad just pulled up and were two stepping up the drive. I can see the excitement in their faces. No fear for these two. Brad has his struggles with regular school as well as summer school, and this day of graduation means the struggle is over for now. Angela will soon be in a foreign country where children sometimes go without food and live in make shift houses made of tin with cardboard floors. Seeing these things right in your face, instead of on the TV, will rip your heart right out of your chest. When poverty is in your face like this, it's hard to feel sorry for yourself and be depressed, when you live in a great country like the United States of America. This may be the thing that shakes Angela right out of her depression. Brad is just happy that he gets $5000 to go towards his education when he is done helping in the foreign countries. He is all excited about his future of fighting crime as a DEA agent. Brad gets a high from helping people, that's why the Peace Core is perfect for him.

Next to arrive is BreAnna and Jake. They are the perfect couple. No worries for these two with their scholarships. Some people just live a charmed life. I've always heard that those who struggle have a greater appreciation for what they achieve, I guess I'll find out in the next few years of struggles to pay for my college. BreAnna and Jake have their arms around each other as they walk up the driveway. As I look at them all the memories are flashing before me of the days when I first met each of them. How they were my friends separate from each other. Jake was my tutor for Algebra and BreAnna was my sidekick in basketball. How when I introduced them to each other and it was love at first sight. How I felt lost when they were so wrapped up in each other, and I felt like an outsider. Two's company three's a crowd. How I was forced to make new friends, and as a result, all these wonderful people at this party are my best friends. Things just have a way of working out.

BreAnna and Jake grabbed me and we had a group hug. Jake said, "This is a awesome day." He kissed me on the cheek and I kissed him back on his cheek. The nerd that helped me with my algebra years ago has the highest grades of all the seniors. He gave the farewell speech at our graduation today and I'm proud to say he's my friend.

Last to arrive is Kyle. When he got out of his car he grabbed Sara and swung her in a circle. She was squealing with excitement. Kyle graduated from his smart kids school today also. He popped his trunk open and pulled out an electric piano. He's going to show off his talents today. I'm so excited that Kyle is giving us a private concert. He has a bright future in music and has just released his first single, and we will be the first people to see him perform his new song.

Excitement is filling the air. Everyone seems so grown up today. It is the feeling of accomplishment that has all of us strutting around like we are somebody. Jake demanded our attention; "I want to make a toast to our future. I have one thing to say, 'Birds of a feather flock together,' friends forever." We all raised our glasses in agreement. "One more thing, 'Always remember that our government is suppose to work for us, not us support the government,' somehow I forgot to say that in my speech today." Zack yelled, "That's what I'm talking about. You made a great speech for graduation. This is even a greater speech right now. I'll toast to that." We all raised our glasses and this time touched the rim to each others glass in total agreement.

A romantic song began to play and BreAnna and Jake began to dance. We all followed suit and good vibes filled the air. I thought, how lucky we are to have each other as friends. Seldom do friends stay together for this long. I hope we last a lifetime.

Zack is holding me close and I'm melting into his arms. We are both light on our feet and floating to the music. It seems magical, like a fairy tale, or like I would image what is happening and add to the intensity in my mind. When I open my eyes I realize this is real, what I'm feeling is happening right now and I must accept that my feelings are real. Is this what love feels like or is this just a major crush that I'm feeling? I wonder why my senses are so heightened, like how I can smell Zack's clothes. They have been dried on a line outside. Clothes that dry outside in the wind have a fresh smell all their own. What I'm feeling is like my nostrils are opening up bigger than ever before in my life and my breath is deeper than my lungs are big. My eyes are seeing Zack clearer than ever before. My body is light as a feather. I can feel my hair brush against my shoulders as we turn quickly. I seem to be aware of every movement and motion, taking place like it is exaggerated. It's like an out of body experience. I wonder if Zack is feeling what I'm feeling. While those thoughts were going through my head, Zack kissed my neck. Goose bumps fill my entire body. I'm melting, will someone please scoop me up off the floor.

The last time Sara had a party we had chaperones. I see why now. This time Sara's parents are going out to eat and than to a movie. They are expected to be home around midnight. I take it to mean we are considered mature enough to take care of ourselves or that they trust us. That is nice.

We all danced until we needed a break. Sara suggested we draw for the short toothpick for a new word to add to our vocabulary. Jake volunteered to give the meaning of the new word and broke off a toothpick to be the short toothpick drawn. We all drew a toothpick and Kyle drew the short one. Kyle gave the word electrocoagulation, and Jake just shrugged his shoulders. Zack said, "I know the meaning of electrocoagulation, it is the use of a high frequency electric current to coagulate and destroy tissue. My dad is a doctor and taught me that word." Jake said, "I spoke to soon on giving the meaning, I guess all the attention on my smarts today went to my head. Good job Zack." Kyle gave a smug smile, like I got you.

I looked at Zack with a smile all over my face and nodded like, 'You go Zack.' Sara said, "I don't know if we will use that word or not. Looks like our future doctor will but I don't know about the rest of us. Anyway it's time for us to give advice that will help us in the future. I would like to start with, 'It's more important to be beautiful on the inside than to be just beautiful to look at and be a monster on the inside. Your beautiful soul is what you take with you when you leave this world. Guard your soul for it is forever, it is the real you. Our bodies are the temples of the Lord. What you do to your body you do to the Lord.' You guys saved me from making a big mistake earlier this year and I thank you for it."

Kyle said, "That was beautiful, thank you for sharing it with us, Sara. I would like to extend your thought with a similar word of advice. 'You must be rooted in love in order to look into one's heart for love and not be fooled by the beauty on the outer shell of the person you are looking at. The heart is where affection lives. God gave me the ability to do this because I live for God and He gift's me with this knowledge. I live in the consciousness of God, which brings awareness in my heart. If I question my thoughts I ask myself, 'Would God do this,' before I act on my thoughts. This is how I protect myself. God lives in me and is the power and knowledge that makes me who I have become."

Everyone stood up and clapped their hands. Brad said, "That certainly is something we all can use. Both of you did outstanding. You're a hard act to follow. I'm going to keep it short and to the point. 'Drugs lead to jail, death, or even insanity. They also steal your soul. Help those who enter this nightmare. They need you.' With that I give the floor to Angela."

"You guys are my spiritual directors and I love each of you for it. I would like to share what I have seen with my own eyes. I ask you to make anyone who does this, aware of what they are doing. 'Some people will hurt their family and do some goodie goodie things for strangers, thinking they can make the stranger think they are a good soul. Your family should always be first on your list. You may be able to fool a stranger but you can't fool God. He knows the real you.' With that I ask Chelsea to share something good with us," Angela said.

"I so agree with you on that one Angela. Family is so important. Guard them like they are a treasure chest. They touch you emotionally, so embrace them. So much for that, what I have to share is, 'Don't let Satan take over your tongue.' Not a lot of words but very powerful words, don't you think? Hope you all enjoyed it," I said.

"I guess it's my turn. 'You are what you are, not what you say you are. People can see through your words. You lose your creditability with little white lies. You lose the respect of others and you lose yourself. You are treated differently if you lose your creditability.' I tell you this in case any of you run for a political position. Don't get caught up in the political way of doing things. The splendor of truth will harbor trust," Zack said.

"I like that Zack. Never underestimate the power of truth. I have just one simple little line I would like to share with you. 'Sin can be defined as the rejection of God.' I know it's not long but it speaks volumes. God's word is the Bible and if you live by the Bible you live by God's word." BreAnna said.

"We don't need a long speech when one line says it all. We are saved when we accept God's grace. Good job BreAnna. In Corinthians 2:10-11 Paul, "I have forgiven in the sight of Christ. For your sake, in order that Satan might not outwit us, for we are not unaware of his schemes." We must forgive in order to keep the devil out of our life. If we punish someone by telling others what they did or by making them feel guilty, we are hurting ourselves. A person who lives in fear always wants to punish others. If I am to forgive others, I must first forgive myself. I was born into a state of sin and cannot help sinning, but I also can ask for forgiveness and be forgiven. Let the past be the past.' Very powerful words don't you guys think?" Jake said.

Another standing ovation is in order. Great enthusiasm fills the air, with a prolonged applause. I think we gave an applause that lasted at least one whole minute. We acknowledge each other with a nod, and a look in our eye that says, 'We get it.'

After everyone settled down Sara announced that her very good friend, Kyle, also graduated today with honors in music, and that he brought his portable piano to play his newly recorded piece of music. We truly are blessed to have such a talent among us. We all sat down in anticipation of hearing what kind of creation our good friend Kyle is about to share with us. Kyle has talent to burn, he is just overflowing with goodness and it shows as he begins to play. He has generated a thrill with just the beginning of this piece of music. I began to feel like I did when Zack kissed my neck. Who would have thought music could have such an effect on a person. Kyle has a certain style that glitters in the limelight, and is sweeping all of us off our feet. The flow of each note penetrate our minds, and we become mellow as the essence of his music fills our senses. Our bodies are light as a feather and weak as a kitten. We are under the spell of the music, which right now is representing love. The rhythmic pulse is an acoustical paradise that creates a feeling of clairvoyance into what Kyle is trying to say with his music, 'peace.' As Kyle ended his musical artwork he looked up at us with an electrifying smile as if to say 'you get it, don't you.'

Kyle said, "I want to create my own world of new music. I'm in command of my destiny because God has gifted me with this talent. Music is the essence of enjoyment for me and I hope to create a cultural that brings clarity to the minds of my listeners of why they are here on earth. I want it to be transparent that God loves them and gives them the ability to feel joy."

"You truly are stylistically gifted and you have taken me to a new place in life today. It would have been a daunting enough task for someone at the top of their profession, much less for a seventeen year old kid to produce such a magical piece of music. Your strength and depth of music were in every note of this masterpiece. The passion in you was shared with each one of us. You have broken the musical barrier where different people like different sounds. No longer will people be able to say 'I know I'm getting old when I don't get the music these young people are playing today. It just doesn't sound like the good old music did when we were kids.' All generations will get this new sound. We felt your music, and I thank you for sharing it with us," Jake said.

"The seductive clarity that warrants praise from even the most skeptical listener, such as myself, must tell you how today I have found appreciation for the keyboard," said BreAnna.

The rest of us were left speechless at what we just experienced, and one by one we gave Kyle a hug around his neck with respectful silence.

Kyle will go down in history along with Mozart and Beethoven whose music has a mesmerizing effect on those who listen to it. All can generate a thrill with just a few notes. They will always be fashionable. Kyle's music in my opinion takes his sound a step further; I was hypnotized by his music. Kyle could very well be the most style-setting music maker in modern time, a style that will always be fashionable.

For most fashions, they pass and become antiquated. Years later some may resurface, if the fashion world approves. An Argentinean dance started as an underground movement by the poor called the tango is always in style. The tango is for all ages and exploded all over the world, and has broken the rules of fashion. Kyle will break the time barrier with his music just like the tango upset the fashion world and changed the rules of becoming outdated. Kyle will make this kind of impact in the world of music, and the word I'm looking for is, timeless.

This day will be with me forever, and history has been made before my very eyes. Kyle is on his way to becoming the person responsible for world peace. This is his goal and I believe he is in the process of achieving what he set his mind to. The tranquility that filled my body as I listened to Kyle play his piece of music made me aware that I was listening to a genius, an exceptional intellectual and creative power. When Kyle shares this music with the world, it will be filled with serenity, and ultimately become a better life for all, peaceful.

Sara ordered pizza to be delivered and there were six

boxes. She wanted to be sure no one went hungry. The guys didn't waste any time digging in. They drifted off to one side of the room and the girls to the other. Sara felt a need to bring up the subject of Nick. She said, "Nick called me the other day and his wife had a baby girl. They named her Nichole, after Nick. He told me what you guys did for him and apologized to me for what he did to me. You know, how he deceived me. He asked for my forgiveness and is in counseling now. Nick found out through counseling that the more he has at stake the more he risk. It's like an addiction, risking everything in his life made him feel more alive and on the edge. Nick put his family life at risk and only became aware of it when my good friends forced an end to his destructive behavior. You guys brought the deep penetration of reality upon him. You brought him out of the trance he was in. He told me that now he is surrounded by a tenaciously lingering thought of what his life could be if he learns to discipline his mind. He told me the path of God is in his relationship with his wife now. His marriage is stronger now because he is concerned about what is good for his marriage instead of what is good for his pleasure. Pleasure is a two way street and now he ask himself how can he create pleasure for his marriage. Nick stumbled; he has straightened up his life and is grateful that you guys forced him back into God's grace, before he fell flat on his face. He said, "Our love for God is love for others, it is selfless, I was selfish in the worst of ways, I could have damaged you and I apologize for that and hope you accept. Your friends saved me from hell, the sense of guilt that would never go away, from shaming my family. I love my family and often read the Bible to reinforce what is important to me. One of my favorite lines is in John 4:16, "God is love. Who ever lives in love lives in God, and God in him." I have acknowledged sin and now I move on in life, and I have learned from my sins." I told Nick that my favorite prayer is The Lords Prayer, and my favorite line is 'forgive us our trespasses as we forgive those who trespassed against us.' You can defeat the devil with total forgiveness," Sara said.

"Sara, I'm so sorry we didn't tell you. We wanted to spare you the pain. We hoped Nick would just disappear. I hope you can forgive us for our silence," I said. "You guys handled it perfect. No need to cause anyone unnecessary pain," Sara said.

The guys were playing pool as we joined them to see who was winning. Jake was about to make the last shot on the table and was rambling something about playing pool is just one's ability to make measurements, and relationships of points, lines, angles, surfaces, and solids. As he finished mumbling, the last ball fell into a pocket.

BreAnna said, "Jake, would you like a partner, we can take on a couples game, will call it 'last couple standing,' we will draw straws for who gets to start." Jake nodded his head in agreement. The first couple to take Jake and BreAnna on is Brad and Angela. Neither has played pool before and it did not last long. Needless to say they were the first couple to be eliminated. Next in line was, Zack and myself. We lasted longer but we also were no match for Jake and BreAnna. Last but not least are Sara and Kyle. Now this is a game to behold. Sara plays pool on a regular basis and she is shinning right now. She has Jake scratching his head while he is making his mathematical equations in his head. Somehow, Sara is just sinking those balls in the pockets with the greatest of ease. She is not leaving any easy shots on the table, and this is making it very difficult for Jake. Each shot is carefully calculated, Jake is eyeballing the direction his cue stick is pointing, and if it looks a little off he jumps in another direction and points the stick again until he thinks he has the perfect shot.

This game has come down to just two players. Jake with his mathematical genius method and Sara with her two years of experience of playing pool. Sara would set up shots for fun to see if she can make it for the past two years and practice is paying off. This gave her a lot of experience. BreAnna and Kyle, Zack and myself, Angela and Brad, we are just taking up space. We are watching and enjoying what real competition in pool looks like. This game has come down to Jake and Sara and friendship is gone out the window, they are both out for blood. It's war, and all is fair in love and war. This six-pocket billiard table has gone from 15 balls down to seven. Jake has four stripped balls on the table and Sara has three solid balls on the table, and its Sara's shot. Sara is sitting on the table with her cue stick behind her back, is she showing off her talent, or does she need to be sitting on the table in order to line up the cue ball with the green solid ball she is fixing to attempt to put in a side pocket. Whatever the case she made the shot, and the room became dead silent. Next she is lining up the red solid ball. There is no way she can make the shot without banking the cue ball clear to the other end of the table. As it rolls back to the end of the table where Sara is standing, it should just barely kiss the red ball so only it goes in the pocket. She doesn't want the cue ball to drop in the pocket, it would be called a scratch ball and that would make it Jake's turn to play. Sara is taking her time and laying her cue stick on the top of the table, but not touching the table or the ball. Sara is using visual means to put the ball into the pocket where if it were Jake's turn to shoot, he would be calculating in his brain how to get it in the pocket. Sara just measures with her stick.

Sara draws back her cue stick and practices the shot by coming close to the cue ball but not striking it. This goes on for quite some time and then Sara stops and places her cue stick above the spot where she plans to bank the cue ball. Then where she thinks the cue ball will hit the bank and then the red ball. She will have to hit the cue ball with some force in order to get it all the way from one end of the table to the other. Sara begins to line up her stick once again to strike the cue ball. She draws it back and lets it slide through her fingers to strike the cue ball, and the stick follows through as

Sara goes from a crouched position to standing straight up. The cue ball strikes the bank, rolls back towards where Sara is standing right past Jakes balls, that were responsible for this difficult shot in the first place, and strikes the red ball. The red ball falls into the pocket and the cue ball is right on the edge of the pocket. I believe if anyone were to blow on it, it would fall right into the pocket with the red ball. Sara takes some time out to take a drink of lemonade. The room is in complete silence once again. You could hear a pin drop. Sara leans over the table and lines up her stick. She draws it back and begins rocking it back and forth and strikes the cue ball with just enough force to put the purple ball in a side pocket with just a tap on the very edge of the ball. Now it's time for the eight ball. Jake looks like a beaten man. It's showing all over his face as Sara calls and points to the corner pocket. This last shot is so simple even I could make it. Sara strikes the cue ball and turn's to celebrate before the ball even falls into the pocket. That's how much confidence she has in her ability to sink it. She puts her hands up for Kyle to give her a high five. Kyle still has his eye on the ball as he raises his hand in the air. Their hands connect just as the ball drops into the pocket.

What I have learned by observing this game is that experience trumps genius. Hand eye coordination, talent, and two years of practice gives Sara the advantage. This proves that practice at whatever, gives one an edge over their opponent just like BreAnna preaches to us when it comes to soccer.

Once again the girls went their way and the guys continued to play pool. Not to boast, in front of the guys after Sara showed the guys how to play pool, when we were out of their sight, high fives were being slapped with great vigor.

BreAnna said, "Jake needed to be brought back down to earth, he is flying a little to high for his own good, however, Jake is spot on about how we have to get involved with government and laws and knowing who to put in office to reflect our values. We could lose out freedom little by little while we are young by not getting involved in politics and putting the right people in power. I began reading the Bible this morning, Romans 7:7-12, 'Yet it was only through the law that I came to know sin. I should never have known what evil desire was unless the law said, "You shall not covet." Sin seized that opportunity; it used the commandment to rouse in me every kind of evil desire. Without law sin is dead, and at first I lived without law. Then the commandment came; with it sin came to life, and I died. The commandment that should have led to life brought me death. Sin found its opportunity and used the commandment: first to deceive me, than to kill me. Yet the law is holy and the commandment is holy and just and good.' That is why we need good laws.

The government has to make laws to keep people in line because not everyone believes in God and reads the Bible. When you read, "You shall not covet," this means you should not want what you see that others have. You become a prisoner of your desires or you become a thief and steal and become a prisoner of sin. In other words, to 'covet,' is a, lose, lose situation.

Another, Romans 13:9-10 'You shall love your neighbor as yourself. Love never wrongs the neighbor, hence love is the fulfillment of the law.' This is my favorite. If everyone could live this way, we would have a lot of empty prisons.

Sara, I ran across a passage I know you will like, Romans 14:1-4 'Extend a kind welcome to those who are weak in faith. Do not enter into disputes with them. A man of sound faith knows he can eat anything, while one who is weak in faith eats only vegetables. The man who will eat anything must not ridicule him who abstains from certain foods; the man who abstains must not sit in judgment on him who eats. After all, God Himself has made him welcome. Who are you to pass judgment on another's servant? His master alone can judge whether he stands or falls.'

Chelsea and Angela, the passage I thought the two of you would most relate to is, Romans 16:17-20 'Brothers, I beg you to be on the watch against those who cause dissension and scandal, contrary to the teaching you have received. Avoid their company. Such men serve, not Christ our Lord, but their own bellies, and they deceive the simpleminded with smooth and flattering speech. Your obedience is known to all, and so I am delighted with you. I want you to be wise in regard to what is good and innocent of all evil. Then the God of peace will quickly crush Satan under your feet. May the grace of our Lord Jesus Christ be with you.'

I had to share that with you today, it was just inside me and I had to get it out. Emotions are in the air because soon we will all be going our own way, but if we keep God close to our hearts we will all be just fine. I know we will be in each other's hearts, even if miles of distance, is between us. If you start missing me, just close your eyes and remember all the good times we have had together. That's the beauty of our mind; we can put whatever we want in them. I know when we all have our college behind us we will come back home to start our new lives. Let's enjoy the journey and keep God next to our hearts, with Him we will be just fine."

Angela said, "Thanks for sharing that with us, BreAnna, I have something I've been studying in the book of Revelation. We all know that I have a tendency to gravitate to the dark side of life, but I'm going to share with you what I have committed to memory. It is Revelation 20:1-20, 'Then I saw an angel come down from heaven, holding the key to the abyss and a huge chain in his hand. He seized the dragon, the ancient serpent, who is the devil or Satan, and chained him up for a thousand years. The angel hurled him into the abyss, which he closed and sealed over him. He did this so that the dragon might not lead the nations astray until the thousand years are over. After this, the dragon is to be released for a short time.

Then I saw some thrones. Those who were sitting on them were empowered to pass judgment. I also saw the spirits of those who had been beheaded for their witness to Jesus and the word of God, those who had never worshiped the beast or its image nor accepted its mark on their foreheads or their hands. They came to life again and reigned with Christ for a thousand years. The others who were dead did not come to life till the thousand years were over. This is the first resurrection; happy and holy are they who share in the first resurrection! The second death will have no claim on them; they shall serve God and Christ as priests, and shall reign with him for a thousand years.

When the thousand years are over, Satan will be released from his prison. He will go out to seduce the nations in all four corners of the earth, and muster for war the troops of Gog and Magog, numerous as the sands of the sea. They invaded the whole country and surrounded the beloved city where God's people were encamped; but fire came down from heaven and devoured them. The devil who led them astray was hurled into the pool of burning sulphur, where the beast and the false prophet had also been thrown. There they will be tortured day and night, forever and ever.' I know this sounds scary, but hell is a very scary place. It's a place that I avoid at all cost. By not putting my head in the sand and not ignoring the fact that hell exist, I'm able to assure a spot for myself in heaven. That is my goal, a straight shot to heaven and knowing that I will get there."

Sara said, "The passage that has a lot of meaning to me is John 8:1-11, 'While Jesus went out to the Mount of Olives, at daybreak he reappeared in the temple area; and when the people started coming to him he sat down and began to teach them. The scribes and the Pharisees led a woman forward who had been caught in adultery. They made her stand there in front of everyone. "Teacher," they said to him, "This woman has been caught in the act of adultery. In the law, Moses ordered such women to be stoned. What do you have to say about the case? (They were posing this question to trap him, so that they could have something to accuse him of.) Jesus bent down and started tracing on the ground with his finger. When they persisted in their questioning, he straightened up and said to them, "Let the man among you who has no sin be the first to cast a stone at her." A second time he bent down and wrote on the ground. Then the audience drifted away one by one, beginning with the elders. This left him alone with the women, who continued to stand there before him. Jesus finally straightened up and said to her, "Woman where did they all disappear to? Has no one condemned you?" "No one sir," she answered. Jesus said, "Nor do I condemn you. You may go. But from now on, avoid this sin." After the episode with Nick, I began looking for answers, and this was it. Hope you all enjoyed it."

I said, "Well I guess you all want to hear what I have to add to this conversation. Because Jeff had a near death experience and I went to the bottom of the river and also came close to death, I've given death some thought now and than and I would like to share a passage from Hebrew that I read often. Hebrews 2:14-18, 'Now since the children are men of blood and flesh, Jesus like wise had a full share in ours, that by his death he might rob the devil, the prince of death, of his power, and free those who through fear of death had been slaves their whole life long. Surely he did not come to help angels, but rather the children of Abraham; therefore he had to become like his brother in every way, that he might be a merciful and faithful high priest before God on their behalf, to expiate the sins of the people. Since he was himself tested through what he suffered, he is able to help those who are tempted.' I did become fearful of death when Jeff was lying in the hospital in a coma for so long.

I was looking death right in the eye and became fearful of death. I searched the Bible for answers and realized my fear had enslaved me, and I ask God to help me overcome my feelings, and He did."

The guys were discussing government when we joined the conversation. Zack was talking about entitlement programs, a government program that guarantees and provides benefits to a particular group. He started off with the farmers who are paid not to grow certain crops as his first topic. Right now he is discussing corn. Zack said, "Farmers are paid to plant corn, and corn syrup is put into many foods as a sweetener, and that is one of the main causes of obesity in this country. Than we give the poor these credit cards to buy food high in corn syrup which we know is a hazard to our health. Products made with corn syrup are very cheap because the government subsidizes the farmer, who grows the corn. The family that grows up eating all this corn syrup becomes very fat, and fat creates health issues like heart trouble, then the government subsidizes the very people they made fat, with healthcare. I say, if the government subsidizes the farmers to grow greens and other healthy vegetables so the poor can afford to feed their family on healthy foods, we could most all live longer and die of old age, instead of going to the hospital because of unhealthy life styles and dieing a slow death. How about letting the poor pick up healthy food from a restaurant, to go, that will feed their families and let them put it on the credit food card. As long as it is healthy and affordable they should be able to use the food card to feed their families. An example of a restaurant to go dinner would be, baked chicken for your protein, brown rice and beans for the perfect amino acid that feeds the brain, and broccoli for the calcium for your bones and teeth, and cantaloupe for desert. Water is very healthy for the drink. They could use this food card to pay for a balanced meal for the whole family. I believe the price of health care would go down considerable."

Brad said, "Another problem with our government is the drug war. It just keeps getting worse. You have the lawyers who get the drug dealer off so they can continue to deal drugs, and if they go to prison sometimes they run their business from prison. It's like we are just spinning our wheels. We need to find a way to put the drug dealers out of business. They are ruining our youth. We risk total collapse of our nation if our youth continue to destroy their brains. The stuff out their today is very hazardous, and our youth think they are invincible. If counseling on behavior became a class all must take, we could prevent the cause of why children risk drug use. We need highly skilled councilors who know how to stop a runaway train and put it back on the right track."

Jake said, "In my opinion, we need to bring back the class of civics like my grandparents had. The study of civics is the branch of political science concerned with civic affairs. Teens now days don't know how a city is run. I believe if civics is made mandatory, required, and part of getting a passing grade would be to write a paper on ways to improve civic affairs, we could all benefit from their suggestions. This class would let them know how things are run and knowledge is power, and power creates interest, and interest solves problems. I believe the parents of most teens are two busy trying to put food on the table and clothes on their back to be concerned with what's being taught in school. There are better ways to run the state, and government, and bringing young minds into the equation is the answer.

If employees of the state, the mayor, or legislators, where to visit these classes and discuss what they do all day, such as some of the problems, and solutions to these problems, were shared and discussed with the students, the process of how the state is run would be better understood by the students. Because civic is not taught, most students don't know how the state is run."

Kyle said, "School is the place to make changes. The mindset needs to be in place and student need time to adjust. Business needs to be taught, not just talked about, but put in place. Not everyone can afford to go to college so high schools need to get students ready for the workplace. A simulated call center job for students to actually perform the duty of the job would make them ready for the workforce the day after they graduate. Many just need to have the confidence of how things work. So many of our call center jobs have gone over seas just because we don't have a workforce ready to step into the position. Knowledge of how things work is power, and we need to empower high school students with the confidence to do the job from day one."

A lot of brainstorming is going on today. We are solving the problems of our country and have only graduated from high school for a few hours, not even a full day. This is what I love about my friends. None are self-consumed about their selves. It's not 'what about me,' it's what can I do to make things better for society as a whole. When you become consumed with I, I, I, you can't see the big picture. If your country is depressed, you will not have as much fun with a bunch of sad people. We must make things as good as possible for our country as a whole. I believe we are living in the promise land, but we are responsible for keeping it beautiful, healthy, and morally sound.

The gathering is over and Sara is walking us to our cars. Thoughts are running through my head that we may soon all be scattering in different directions. It makes me sad to think that the whole high school scene is over. I've had a blast and can't even image anyone dropping out and missing out on what I've experienced. These days I will cherish my entire life. They very well could be the best days of my life. I'm looking forward to college but my friends are being scattered to the wind. We are all going in different directions. I know we will stay in contact over the Internet and on our cell phones, but it won't be the same as touching each other with a hug or a high five. I miss them just thinking about how it's going to be without them on a daily bases.

Zack can tell something is just not right with me. On the drive home he said, "Chelsea are you okay. You seem down in the dumps for some reason." I responded, "Zack it just hit me a while ago that we are all going our separate directions and I just got sad. I can't control how I feel right now. It is overwhelming." Zack said, "I know just how you feel, I'm covering it up but I feel the same way. We celebrated tonight our graduation, and it is something to celebrate, but going out into the world to make our own way without all the free time to enjoy each other's company is a loss. We've had a great run at the whole high school experience and it is sad that it's over, but it will always be something we can draw on when we need a good thought. Let's see if we can muster up a good thought right now to get this sadness to go away. How about the time Brad was in Drivers Ed and the teacher said to him, 'Slow down and I'll jump and take my chances.' That was pretty funny don't you think? Or the time Sara was up on her soap box and the teacher had to escort her back to her seat because she wouldn't stop talking and let anyone else have a turn. She was talking all the way to her seat. Or how about the time BreAnna grabbed the basketball on the court and headed down the wrong end of the court to make a basket, and realized it just in time, and turned around and ran down to the other end of the court only to make the winning score. We have a lot of funny things to make us LOL. Don't you think?" We both started laughing and my mood lightened. It's nice to know I'm not the only one affected by the future.

Chapter 13

Cupid Strikes

I'm being hit by a bow and arrow from both sides. Jeff is
E-Mailing every other day and remembers some of the time
we had together in Florida. Jeff still holds me at bay, like he
is being very careful not to lead me on, but at the same time
I can feel his joy when we talk.

Ed keeps Jeff busy with home schooling and church
events. Jeff is getting where he can be around people for
longer periods of time without having panic attacks. He is
off all medicine and Ed thinks in another year Jeff will be
back to his old self. Jeff told me he would like to visit me
this summer and swim in the pond. He thinks it looks like a
little piece of paradise on earth. I thought to myself, thank
goodness the apple tree is in the backyard and not by the
pond. Don't need an Adam and Eve rerun.

Zack visits me regularly and all who know us considers
us boyfriend and girlfriend, but we have not commitment
to one another. It's an unspoken relationship that we both
cherish. Zack knows that Jeff contacts me on a regular basis,
however he never mentions it to me. He is so sure of himself
that he even asks me on occasion how Jeff is doing.

We have a soccer game this afternoon and Zack is picking
me up to take me to the game. He enjoys watching the girls
play. I made Jeff a promise, an assurance, that I would not
use my head to hit the ball with, unless it would be the only

way to make points on the board. Jeff just doesn't want me to take any chances of what happened to him to possible happen to me. Neither would I.

The Elite Kickers are on the field when Zack pulled into the parking lot. We got hung up in traffic or I would be out their with them right now. When I began to walk on the field, BreAnna spotted me and tapped Angela and Sara on the shoulder and they jogged over to meet me. "Where have you been?" said BreAnna. I explained we got stuck in traffic. BreAnna briefed me about our opponents as we walked towards the Elite Kickers.

"The goalkeeper is very tall so we need to try to score on the ground. As a general rule with tall people, the upper half of their body works better than the lower half. Anyway that's what it looks like with this goalkeeper. She seems to be weakest on her left side. Her team is working to strengthen this weakness by kicking the ball to her over and over again. We can take these Jaybirds down by putting the ball in the goal on the left side," BreAnna said.

The guys are all setting together on the front row cheering us on. BreAnna is doing a great job of blocking the ball that the Jaybirds are kicking high, low and up the middle. The first half of the game has resulted in a zero to zero score. The coach is encouraging us to keep up the good work and get a little closer to the goal while keeping the ball on the ground. The Jaybirds goaltender is weak on the ground balls and you must always attack the weak spot. Our coach has a good eye for finding a vulnerable spot, which leads a team to being susceptible to attack in that area. Angela and Sara started plotting on just how to score. Angela said, "Sara I'm going to get the ball close to the left side of the field and then take the ball up the field toward their goal, turn and than kick it behind me where you will take over and give the ball a side kick into the goal. We will get these Jaybirds completely off guard and score."

It sounds like a good plan and I will stay close to Sara to

make sure none of the Jaybirds can steal the ball during this play. The halftime is over and it's time to put a score on the board. The Jaybirds have control of the ball first and they are pumped up. The ball is being passed among them like they are the only ones on the field; I've never seen anything like it. Every move they make is perfect. It's as if the Elite Kickers are not even on the field, like we are invisible. The ball is to high when it is in the air and to fast when it is on the ground. They are heading to the goal at increasing speed, the ball is in the air, heading to the net when BreAnna leaps into the air and blocks the ball. Now the ball is under my foot and I kick it to Angela. She is keeping the ball close to her feet as she nears the goal. Suddenly she turns around just like we planned. She kicks the ball behind her and Sara strikes the ball with the shoelaces of her shoe but the goalkeeper blocks her shot. The ball veers off in my direction, as I throw my leg back so my kick can have the power it needs, I strike the ball with full force. When I connected with the ball my foot followed through and I was full bodied on the ground. I've never kicked with such force and as I watched the ball, while lying on the ground, a rush filled my body as the ball passes right past the goalkeeper and into the net. My eyes go straight to Zack as I can hear him yelling my name and I see him jumping into the air with his fist reaching for the sky. As I put my feet under me and rise I catch myself jumping for joy, knowing that I just put a point on the board.

The end score is one to zero. My parents grabbed me as I left the field and we had a group hug. Mom said, "This calls for a celebration. Chelsea, why don't you invite all your friends over and me and your dad will charcoal some burgers? We will stop by the store; you and your friends can hit the freig and have some fresh lemonade I made this morning.

There is a convoy heading for my house. BreAnna and Jake are leading, Zack and myself are behind them and following us is Angela and Brad then Sara and Kyle. It is a warm summer day and the lemonade is hitting the spot. Zack suggested we head for the pond for a dip. When we arrived, there was Bam and Boo getting a drink of water. Everyone is giving 'ah's, at what a cute fawn,' when they saw Boo. BreAnna said, "Look at the little white spots on Boo's back. She is adorable."

The guys took off their shirts and shoes and jumped in with just their shorts and undeis on. All of us girls removed our shoes and jumped in with our soccer uniforms. The spring feed pond is crystal clear today and this adds to the excitement. It truly is a little piece of paradise here on earth.

The pond is very deep and each of the guys dived in to see if they could touch the bottom, which is in the center of the pond. Each one gave it their all but no one could reach the bottom. Brad said, "This pond must be coming from the center of the earth. It is like a bottomless pit." We all got a chuckle out of Brad's inability to succeed in finding the bottom, because in his mind he can conquer about anything. Jake said, "I started diving where I could touch the bottom and keep my hands on the rocks as I descended but my ears were about to pop so I had to come up. It is really dark down there. I wonder if there are any monster fish in that deep dark hole. Next time I will bring a light. I might even bring a spear incase something gets after me." This scared Sara and she got out of the water in a hurry. I said, "Come on Sara, I've been swimming in this pond all my life and nothing ever got me. Get back in."

We were splashing around for a while and using the rope that is tied to the tree to drop off in the deep part of the pond, when mother called us to eat with the ringing of the bell. She loves to ring this large bell when supper is ready, it makes her feel like she is demanding we all come to the supper table at once, and we do.

My friends and me are walking right behind each other

in a single file dripping all the way. Mother insisted we shower off in the out door shower just in case any bugs got on us. The burgers smell heavenly. Dad is putting slices of cheese on each burger and warming the top bun. Mother is spreading mustard on the bottom bun and putting a slice of onion on top of the mustard, than pickles, a slice of tomato, and than lettuce. Ten paper plates have the bottom buns with the trimming ready for dad to top them off with a burger. We each take a plate and line up for our charcoal burger. Dad really enjoys cooking his oversize burgers and watching the faces of those who are about to indulge. Everyone has a happy look when the burger is placed on top of all the trimmings.

Dinner was wonderful and everyone is having a blast being together. BreAnna stood up to make a toast, "The person responsible for our win today is Chelsea Songbird and I want to make a toast to the move she put on those Jaybirds today. When I seen her leg follow through after she struck the ball, and she was on her butt on the ground, I knew she gave it everything she had. That ball had to be a score and I seen it before it went into the net. Chelsea's determination and hitting that ball with everything she has, won the game." Everyone raised his or her glasses in the toast and I felt my cheek's getting pink. Zack said, "Speech, speech, we want to know how it felt." I stood up and started off with, "Awesome! We all know however, there is no I in the word team. If Angela hadn't set the ball up perfect and Sara hadn't knocked down that Jaybird player by accident none of this would have happened. Let's don't forget that BreAnna saw the Jaybirds weakness and set the play up. I want to make a toast to the team that put me in position to make a score." We all made another toast.

Mom and Dad went into the house to watch TV, and my friends all went home except Zack. We went back to the pond, sat on the bench and just enjoyed God's beautiful artwork called nature. Somehow it feels spiritual to look at all the beauty God has put on this little piece of earth. The butterflies are going from one wild flower to another and their color's range from blue to orange and some are brown with just a touch of gold. A praying mantis, which is a green and brownish predatory insect, set's on the bench with us, folds it's front legs as if in prayer of thanks for all the beauty God has created. A yellow and black meadowlark bird clutches onto a long stem of wild grass and sings a sweet song.

Our eyes are taking in all this beauty as we sit in complete silence. Suddenly a small turtle crawls across my foot and looks up at me as if to say, 'pick me up,' and I did. "Hey little fellow, what's you doing? Where are your mom and dad? You sure are cute," I said. As I reach to touch the top of the turtle's head he pulls back and tucks his head into his shell and closes it tightly. Zack said, "He must be shy." About a minute later he pee's all over my foot. "It's time to put you down, I think you are trying to tell me something," I said. Zack is creaking up as I go to the side of the pond to wash off the turtle pee. That little fellow broke our moment of silence.

Zack picked the turtle up and now he has all four legs going every which way and his neck is out as far as possible. Zack said, "Give the little fellow a kiss. He has his head out all the way." He is adorable so I blew him a kiss. Didn't want to get to close, he might bite my nose off next. Just can't trust the little fellow after he peed on me.

"I got really excited when you kicked that soccer ball and put the only point on the board. It has me looking at soccer in a complete different way. I'm starting to see how billion's people get all wrapped up in this sport. I'm going to be following you around like a groupie, you are my rock star soccer player," Zack said. "Your so sweet, I like it when you come to the games. You are an inspiration for me. I get excited when you holler 'Go Chelsea,' and I can feel myself getting stronger. In other words, you inspire me. I can feel your positive emotion and the result is pure energy that fuels my foot when it connects on the ball. I really focus when playing soccer and it's important that I give it my all because it is my belief that sports are a gift from God. I excel at sports because God gave me the ability to excel. I want to thank you Zack for being a part of what makes me happy. Soccer is part of my destiny and I draw an immense amount of pleasure from the game. I don't have to be the best player on the field but it's nice when I am. It feels good to know that you are in the stands watching me play," I said.

The whole time I was up on my soapbox, Zack was looking me right in my eyes. I feel a great connection with Zack today, even more than normal. I would like to kiss him, but instead grab his hand and start walking towards the house. Now that Jeff is contacting me on a regular basis, I must be careful not to lead Zack on. I would never purposefully hurt the people I care about. In my eyes, that would make me a bad person, and the destruction of a wonderful relationship would be the end result. I want Zack to be a part of my life forever whatever level we wind up on. However I find myself being more and more attracted to Zack. I just don't know if he see's me as just a friend or more than just a friend.

After Zack left I went to check my E-Mails and sure enough Jeff left me a message. In his message he asked if he could come to Oklahoma and see me on my birthday, seeing how I will soon be eighteen. He said that Ed would bring him down if it is okay with me, and they will get a motel room just like last time they were here. My heart skipped a beat as I turned off my computer and savored the moment. My thoughts are all over the place. Can a girl possible care about two boys at the same time? When I make my choice, who will it be, Zack or Jeff?

Sleep is not coming to me tonight. I'm torn between two wonderful people that I care deeply about. I know Zack will accept whatever my decision is, but I'm not sure weather Zack or Jeff is the right person for me to give my heart to. I will have to make a decision after Jeff goes home for I cannot deal with the way I feel right now. Stress is unhealthy and that is what is keeping me awake tonight. I must make a choice between the two and let my crush fall upon only one.

The End

References:

1)   Riverside Webster's II New College Dictionary
2)   Holy Bible